MW00326137

Life Interrupted

*Sharing Trials, Victories,
and the Love of God*

By:

Pam Espinosa

Life Interrupted

Sharing Trials, Victories, and the Love of God

By:

Pam Espinosa

Copyright © 2016, All Rights Reserved
Printed in The United States of America

Published By:

ABM Publications

A division of Andrew Bills Ministries Inc.

PO Box 6811, Orange, CA 92863

www.abmpublications.com

ISBN: 978-1-931820-71-4

All scripture quotations, unless otherwise indicated are taken from the King James Version of the Bible, Public Domain. All rights reserved.

DEDICATIONS

I dedicate this book first and foremost to my Heavenly Father who has loved me when I was so unlovable. Who took me by the hand and walked with me through every trial. Who encouraged me and strengthened me when I did not have anything to give. Who held me in His arms and let me lean up against His chest to feel His loving arms wrap around me as He whispered to me, "Fear not". Who settled my heart to trust in His heart and His love. Who gave me grace for the day, one day at a time.

To my husband, Michael. You showed unconditional love and support for me on a daily basis. You never missed one doctor appointment or treatment, and you never complained. You encouraged me and supported me on a daily basis. You held me tightly in your arms every single night. You prayed for me and with me every day. You fought this fight with me, never giving up. I love you so incredibly much, Babe.

To my kids, Kristin, Michael, Krista, Kehlie, and Kyle. I am blessed beyond words. You all stood beside me and fought for me. Sometimes you would cuddle with me on the couch or the bed and other times you would talk with me on the phone when you could not come over. You were consistent with your love and I felt it daily. I could not ask for better kids to go through this season with, who would love me and encourage me and fight alongside me. I love you all so much.

To my grandbabies. Yes, you were young but you filled me with such joy and laughter and love. You drew me pictures and hung them on my wall so I could see them from my bed. You cuddled me on the couch or the bed. You rubbed my bald head and asked a million questions. You said the funniest things from such a sincere heart. I love you so much.

To my parents, Dave and Zelma Wyatt. You stood beside me and held my hand at every treatment, and stayed to help care for me every week of treatment. I am blessed beyond words for your encouragement, your strength, and your steadfast love for me. You taught me to have faith in God and I don't know where I would be if you did not instill those values into my heart and my life. I love you so much.

To my sisters and brothers on both sides of my family. There is no "in law" – you truly all are my sisters and brothers. There are no words to express my gratitude for your continued love and support through this season of my life. I love each and every one of you.

To my friends. You guys rock my world. I was amazed and overwhelmed by your love and your faithfulness. You brought dinners for months on end. You came and hung out with me almost daily. You offered to shave your head when I had to shave mine. You hired cleaners to come clean my house for me because you know I am a freak about a clean house.

You would visit me at the treatment center. You picked me up when I had anxiety. You would lie on the couch and watch a movie with me even when you knew I would only fall asleep. You showed me the heart of God and I am forever grateful. I love each and every one of you.

To my pastors Jim and Deborah Cobrae, who came to visit me, pray for me, and encourage me in my faith. Your love and devotion was a constant reminder of God's love for me.

I love you all,

Pam

<u>DESCRIPTION</u>

This is a story of Pam's trials and victories, and experiencing God's healing, grace, and unconditional love. Pam is very real and raw in sharing this journey of breast cancer – from diagnosis to double mastectomy, from treatments to reconstruction.

This book will have you laughing and crying, and make you very aware of God's faithfulness to every detail of your life. You will find that there are no victories without battles and that tomorrow is a better day.

TABLE OF CONTENTS

FORWARD

I have known Michael and Pam Espinosa for almost twenty years and in that time they have always been an incredible example for my wife, Eve, and me. They have been role models for us in their marriage, the way they raised their children, and the way they have approached ministry. We have always admired the way they engage life with a steady faith in God's love and an overriding confidence in the power of His word. They are, for us and countless others, a constant source of encouragement and inspiration.

The thing about Michael and Pam is that they have a relentless determination to maintain relationships. Where most of us are willing to allow social media to be the medium in which we relate to others, and the excuse of being busy as the reasoning for that, they routinely go out of their way to personally connect with those in their lives. They value relationships and as a result have many deep and abiding friendships that have endured the test of time. This is exactly why so many people were impacted and mobilized when Pam was diagnosed with breast cancer.

Many times Christians have this notion that nothing difficult or challenging is ever supposed to happen to them. We know verses like Romans 8:37 that say, *"Yet in all these things we are more than conquerors through Him who loved us."* Still, it's like we thought we would never be required to conquer anything. We know from scripture that God doesn't make us sick and actually wants us well, but life is filled with opportunities for us to overcome and be victorious. Each situation and every difficulty comes hardwired with its own lessons and blessings. This is why Michael and Pam have become examples to us of how to navigate life's challenges. It could be said that we learn more during hardship than we do when things are easy. After all, David became a General and then a King after facing and defeating Goliath. It seems seasons of great difficulty and uncertainty become the crucible God uses to forge the character of great men and women of faith. In fact, David wrote many of the Psalms in times of great personal distress only to discover again and again that the faithfulness of God never falters and His grace is always sufficient. David learned to sing in the darkness of his trouble and God illuminated his life.

As you read this book you will hear Pam's song. Her story is a song that resonates with the frequency of the finished work of Jesus. This book will inspire you to believe there is hope in every circumstance, beauty even in difficulty, and a way where there once seemed to be no way. Be ready to experience God's peace and provision like never before on the pages that follow.

I read once that our lives are the sum total of our experiences. This book is about the experiences of a woman of great courage and faith as she faces and overcomes breast cancer with her husband, children, family, and friends by her side. This is a story of discouragement and disappointment, and at times the darkness of the valley of the shadow of death, that gave way to the radiant hope found only in Jesus and His unconditional love.

Ken Spicer
Senior Pastor
New Creation Church, Banning, CA

*****

Pam Espinosa's effervescent love for God, life and people has been a constant witness to all who know her. When she was diagnosed with breast cancer her faith and commitment to believe in God's Word came to the forefront and carried her through to victory and healing. This narrative of that journey will be a great encouragement and aid to all who are experiencing difficult days, and will bring hope to see that with God, nothing is impossible to those who will believe.

Deborah Cobrae
Founder and Senior Pastor
The Rock Church and World Outreach Center
San Bernardino, CA

*****

"Life Interrupted" is a magnificent story of how something meant to destroy you can bring forth incredible growth and strength when surrendered to the Master's loving hand. Rather than have her faith be daunted with that haunting question, "Why?" Pam doesn't question God's love but rather leans on it entirely and sees Him bring about an even deeper healing and love in her life. One of the things I love about Pam is her unique ability to laugh at herself, being completely transparent; this wonderful quality prevails throughout her story. She will make you cry, make you laugh, and make you aware of the awesome

presence of God's love in every minute detail of your life.

Sue Bryan
Senior Children's Ministry Pastor
The Rock Church and World Outreach Center
San Bernardino, CA

* * * * *

What an amazing portrayal of faith in the midst of a storm. Pam's story is real. I was there during some of her most difficult days. When the enemy attacks we may get knocked back for a moment, but Pam is a woman who caught her breath and chose to move forward in faith. She knew the power of her God then, but today knows it in an even greater and more intimate way than ever before. She will tell you her fight was not easy, but she wouldn't change a thing! From her greatest battle she has emerged victorious and her faith has been made strong. If you need encouragement you don't want to miss this read.

Heather Flores
Senior Pastor
The Rock Church
Riverside, CA

<u>INTRODUCTION</u>

Cancer isn't funny but humor is healing. Singing praises in your midnight hour causes you to realize that there may be sorrow in the night but joy comes in the morning. As someone who has gone through breast cancer (mastectomy, chemotherapy, and reconstruction) and gratefully came out the other side, I have learned firsthand that laughter and praise has its place and it sure helps.

From going bald to losing twenty-five pounds the chemo diet way, humor and praise has been an effective weapon in my fight against this disease that is no respecter of persons. This is not to say that I laughed throughout my whole cancer experience; I didn't. This isn't to say that I sang praises every day, because I didn't. However, I often times found myself encouraging those who came by to cheer me up. I would put them at ease by asking them if they wanted to see my boob-less chest or my bald head. Laughter helps, and so does talking to someone who's "been there."

My prayer is that this book will help someone who is going through breast cancer, and also help those who love them. Faith, hope, praise, and a good dose of laughter can make a great difference in the journey you are now experiencing. Sharing with other women helps diffuse the fear of cancer. Cancer is not a life sentence – it is merely a word.

I also hope this book will encourage women everywhere to get a mammogram today!

Chapter 1

LIFE INTERRUPTED

---

*"Trust in the Lord with all your heart and
lean not on your own understanding."*
Proverbs 3:5

Today marks one year since I heard the words: you have cancer. I still remember those words very clearly as they were spoken to me that Friday morning when my doctor called with the biopsy results.

I had not had any pain. In fact, I went to get my yearly physical when my husband's job had come across hard times and there was a possibility they would be closing the doors to his company had someone not bought them out. I knew I had better get my physical while I had insurance. What ended up happening was not part of my plans.

I went for my yearly physical (which is never fun) when the doctor informed me I would need a mammogram. I went in for my first mammogram on August 4, 2009. I received a call a week later that informing me that I would need a second mammogram. It seemed like they needed me to come in soon, but it took a while until I heard anything concerning the second appointment. My second mammogram was scheduled for August 17, 2009. It was less than a week after that appointment when I received a call that I would need to come in for a biopsy.

I remember not being nervous at all. I knew that God was in control and I chose not to walk in worry or fear. After all, seven years earlier, right after I had my very first mammogram, the results came back showing that I would need a biopsy on my right breast. That biopsy showed no cancer but I had to have a lumpectomy to remove the benign lump. So, on September 8, 2009 when I went in for my biopsy I was not fearful at all. This biopsy was quite painful actually. I don't remember my first biopsy being so painful.

Three days later, on September 11, 2009, on Friday morning at 8:30 a.m. I received a phone call from my primary doctor confirming my biopsy results: YOU HAVE BREAST CANCER.

I was very brave on the phone with my doctor as he told me the results and referred me to the surgeon. However, when we hung up, I stood there in the kitchen feeling speechless to actually hear those words... words no one ever wants to hear. I stood there trying to digest the words that were just spoken over me.

My youngest daughter and I were the only ones home when I received the call with such a negative report. I tried to feel very confident when I went into my daughter's room as she was getting ready for work. I told her what the doctor had just told to me. We looked at each other, started crying, and held each other in a tight embrace. It was then that I told her that the night before, as I was praying and believing God for great reports, I felt like God gave me amazing, supernatural peace. I felt that He shared with me, "You're going to be okay." Now being faced with a journey that is unknown and unwelcomed territory, I told God, "I don't know how to do this journey that is ahead of me but with you Jesus, I can do it!"

I called my husband while he was at work. *How do I say this over the phone to the people I love the most? God help me; give me the strength and the courage to speak confidently.* It was so hard to have to tell him the doctor's report over the phone. My precious husband went quiet on the phone, then, as he pulled his thoughts and his heart together, he told me, "It's okay, we are going to fight this and win. With Christ we can do all things."

I went on to call my other kids. They both took the news so bravely and with courage, telling me it's going to be okay. My next phone call had to be to my parents. My mom was so shocked. I felt for a moment it shattered her faith! But she bounced right back and courageously encouraged me that God is my healer and deliverer and through Him we will face this. It was one of the toughest things I ever had to do!

That same Friday afternoon I was in the surgeon's office. As he showed us the findings on the film from the biopsy, we clearly could see what they were identifying as cancer. The surgeon went on to point out other concerns that he had. He feared there was a lot more cancer in the breast that had not yet been biopsied.

Chapter 2

GRACE FOR THE DAY

"Be strong and courageous.
Do not be afraid or terrified because of them,
for the Lord your God goes with you;
He will never leave you nor forsake you."
Deuteronomy 31:6

Monday, September 14, 2009

I was at the hospital to have an MRI. While I was having the MRI, my family, parents, and some close friends were all gathered in the hospital chapel praying over me. I had such peace, peace that surpassed all understanding. As I was going through the MRI, which took approximately forty-five minutes, I was singing praises to God! I felt so incredibly blessed and loved by my family, friends, and most importantly, God!

Wednesday, September 16, 2009

I was back at the hospital to have an ultrasound on my breast. I could tell that the radiologist was concerned. The next day I was back in the surgeon's office. He told me there were three other areas of concern and they would be doing three other biopsies when I went in for my lumpectomy. After speaking with the surgeon, I was off to get my chest X-ray, EKG, and blood work (I am not a needle person!).

This was the first night of Women's Conference at my church. I still went to the conference because, no matter what storm you may be facing, there is nothing like praising God among a group of women. Truly, there is nothing like being in the presence of God; He was turning my valley of trouble into a gateway of hope (Hosea 2:15)!

Friday, September 25, 2009

I went in for my lumpectomy. Although I was nervous, I was at peace while in the waiting room with my family and friends. I was more afraid of the unknown, but I knew that the Lord will never leave me nor forsake me (Deuteronomy 31:6).

In preparation for surgery, they did another ultrasound on my breast. They stuck three very long needles into my breast to locate the other areas they would be checking during the lumpectomy. It was the strangest thing to see these long needles sticking out – a little nauseating, actually! I tried hard to ignore the needles, control my thoughts, and keep my mind focused on God's word.

Once surgery was over, I remember hearing there was no lymph node involvement! I was so excited! At that moment I set in my mind that this meant we were all done with this cancer "stuff."

Wednesday, September 30, 2009

I received a phone call from my surgeon with the news that all three of the biopsies from my lumpectomy were declared cancerous. He stated that my left breast was ridden with cancer. I had Ductal Carcinoma In Situ (DCIS). DCIS is the most common type of non-invasive breast cancer. *Ductal* means the cancer starts inside the milk ducts, *carcinoma* refers to any cancer that begins in the skin or other tissues (including breast tissue) that cover or line the internal organs, and *in situ* means "in the original place."

As well as having DCIS, I was also considered HER2+, which stands for "Human Epidermal growth factor Receptor 2". Her2-overexpressing means there is too much HER2 protein/receptor on the surface of the cancer cells. HER2/neu-positive breast cancer and HER2-overexpressing breast cancer are exactly the same as HER2+ breast cancer. I was HER2+ triple positive, therefore, it was considered invasive and more aggressive.

Friday, October 2, 2009

I was back in the surgeon's office discussing the latest findings. I was told I would need a mastectomy. This news nearly crushed me. I asked the surgeon what the chances were of cancer moving into my right breast. He said it was very high considering how much my left breast was full of cancer. I asked my surgeon what he would tell his wife or mother if they were faced with this decision. He said he can't tell us what to do but he would recommend a double mastectomy. Michael and I took a few days to pray and discuss whether I should have a double mastectomy. Friends were telling me if it were them they would simply have a double mastectomy. I had those same thoughts before now, but found out it's so much harder to make that decision when you are actually facing it. I see nothing "simple" about this decision. *Oh God, you are so faithful. We want to use wisdom and do what is right for us in this situation. Lead us.*

Tuesday, October 6, 2009

We had made the decision to go forward with a double mastectomy. As nervous as I was, I did not want to fear that the cancer could move to my right breast in the future. I also did not want to make a decision based on emotions or fear. I had realized that I could allow fear to paralyze me or motivate me to push through and trust God, replacing my fear with faith.

Once the decision was made to do the double mastectomy I felt supernatural peace, peace that can only come from God Himself. Surgery for the mastectomy was scheduled. *Bittersweet: that's how I feel. Who would want to lose their breast? But then again, who would want to take the chance of cancer coming back in the other one? What would I do without that supernatural peace from God Himself?*

I thought I should try to prepare myself for what was coming, so I looked at online photos of what I would possibly look like after I had the double mastectomy. I felt so overwhelmed with emotions. I will no longer have my breasts! I was "blessed" in this area, so this would be a big change! The pictures I saw looked horrible and did not encourage me at all. I felt that I could only prepare myself so much for what I would really look like with no breasts. Although I did not look forward to the double mastectomy, I did look forward to when I could begin the reconstruction process because that would be a step toward healing.

Chapter 3

DOWN BUT NOT OUT

"Do not grieve,
for the joy of the LORD is your strength."
Nehemiah 8:10b

Wednesday, October 14, 2009

I arrived at the hospital at 6:00 a.m. ready for my surgery. I had such amazing peace. I had a song in my heart. As the nurse was checking my blood pressure he made a comment about my blood pressure being so "normal." He said he never would have known I had cancer and was about to have a double mastectomy based on my blood pressure. God is so good!

Even though I did not have cancer in my right breast, they couldn't do a double mastectomy without first checking the lymph nodes in my right breast. No one had prepared me for what was about to happen, and I will never forget it. The procedure was quite painful. They put about seven shots into my breast and then I had to massage my breast to get the fluid to move into my lymph nodes. After a few minutes of massaging they took pictures to see if the fluid moved into my lymph nodes, and if it had not, then back to more massaging.

The needles were painful, and the massaging was so embarrassing, awkward, and very time-consuming. I thought they should have let my husband help me but that was out of the question. The nurse said if I did not massage my breast adequately she would have to do it, and, well, that motivated me to do a good job! Once this was completed I was ready for my surgery. They would not know lymph node involvement until surgery. *Lymph nodes are part of the immune system. They are found in the neck, behind the ears, in the armpits, and in the chest, belly, and groin.*

While I was waiting for surgery, the hospital waiting room was filling with my family and friends. I was surprised and blessed by all the visitors! I had family and friends coming in to visit me, laugh with me, and pray with me. Every time I thought that was the last person, someone else came in. The man in the surgery waiting area next to me asked me who I was that I would have so many visitors. I told him that I was nobody, but I am just really blessed with a lot of amazing people in my life. God reminded me that I am somebody; I am His and He is taking great care of me.

It was now time to go to in for surgery. The removal of my breasts was soon to be my reality. *Is this really happening right now?* It must be – everyone is here showing support. Even family living far away made the drive to come show their support. *Deep breath.* Hand-in-hand in prayer with my husband, I felt that peace that surpasses all understanding once again. I am trusting in the very one who holds my tomorrow in His hands. *Let's do this!*

Surgery completed, I woke up talking, feeling hungry, and actually feeling great (the effects of great medicine!). My chest was wrapped tightly so it didn't "feel" any different.

My husband, by my side smiling from ear to ear, made my heart jump with joy.

They placed me in a surgery recovery unit that night with five other patients, which made for a very long, sleepless night. I could hear one person sick from their anesthesia, one crying from their pain, one who couldn't breathe because of an anxiety attack, and another trying to get out of bed, delirious from her meds. As I lay there in bed not able to move, now feeling a lot of pain myself, all I could do was pray for everyone I heard having such a hard time. I could have either focused on my own pain, which would have only magnified it, or I could pray for those people who were breaking my heart. That night was a long night and one that I will not soon forget.

When the nurse helped me up to go to the restroom, it was the most excruciating pain I had ever felt. I could not use my arms to get myself up, nor could I use them to use the restroom. The nurse had to help me with everything. The next time I had to use the restroom the nurse brought me a bedpan – not a great idea either. After I used the bedpan the nurse had to clean me up and I felt humiliated that I urinated on myself. I dozed off periodically but never truly slept. Once, a nurse brought me my pain meds and I noticed that it was a different shape than what I had previously been taking. I told him they were not the right pills and after trying to convince me they were, he decided to go check. Sure enough, he almost gave me the wrong meds! I had always been taught to pay attention to what medication you are taking. Thank God I paid attention!

My doctor came to see me first thing in the morning and was I ever so happy to see him. He told me they would have to keep me another night, but in my own room. I pleaded with him to let me go home where I can recover at a much better pace. After some whining on my part he gave in and let me go home. I was so excited to leave the hospital. Little did I know how hard this journey really would be.

Now home and recovering, trying to settle into my new reality, every day was a struggle. Being in pain and not being able to use my arms, I had to rely on everyone for everything (e.g., repositioning me in bed, taking me to the restroom, bathing me, emptying out my drains), and yet every day I felt a supernatural peace that only comes from God. I had a little bell that I rang when I needed my family to come and assist me. Most of the time one of my kids or grandkids would just come and lie in bed next to me or go for walks with me outside to get fresh air. On one hand, this was such a hard time, yet on the other hand it was so rewarding. Sometimes, we are always on the go and don't stay still long enough to enjoy the family around us. I decided to take this time to seek God every day. I asked Him to give me a word that I could hold on to. I asked Him to fill me with His joy knowing that His joy is my strength (Nehemiah 8:10). I had such joy in my heart. Happiness is based on your circumstances; I did not feel happy, but I felt joy unspeakable in the depths of my heart. I had realized that without battles there are no victories and I *am* victorious.

Monday, October 19, 2009

I had my appointment at the surgeon's office and was able to get my drains removed. It was not painful; however, it felt very strange. In a way, I felt free. I felt a little more normal without having drains coming out of my sides. My friend, who is a nurse, came over and bathed me now that my drains were removed. I would not look at myself when she took off the wrap around my chest. I was so afraid of what I would see and did not feel ready for that reality. She shaved my legs, put lotion on me, and then wrapped me back up. It felt so good to have the drains out and feel refreshed after a bath.

Wednesday,
October 21, 2009

My nurse friend came back over to help me shower. After the shower, I told her she didn't need to wrap me back up. I felt ready to see what my new reality looked like. *Deep breath.* I looked in the mirror and was very surprised I didn't look as bad or as ugly as I had 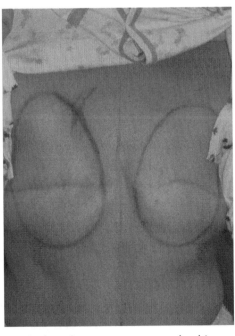 imagined. My surgeon tried to leave me as much skin as he could, and because I was so large-breasted before, I had plenty of skin. It almost looked like I had tiny little breasts. It felt better to see my new reality; I can now start to learn to accept these physical changes. I realized that I actually enjoyed being wrapped up tightly in my bandage because I felt like I had my breasts and a bra on. I slowly began to go without my wrap, and of course had no need for a bra. It slowly began to feel "normal". It certainly was one step at a time and a process that I did not want to have to adjust to. However, I was so glad that I faced my reality. I believe that we must embrace where we are in order to go forward. *This has been easier said than done, but through Christ I can do this.*

I had been praying, asking God to lead me every step of the way in this journey of unknowns and uncharted waters. I prayed for doctors that had the knowledge needed for my specific case, and peace for me for every decision that I needed to make. I was reminded of Mary, the mother of Jesus (Luke 1:26-38). She was young, living her life betrothed to Joseph when an angel appeared to her. She was troubled and the angel told her to not be afraid for she has found favor in the sight of the Lord. He goes on to tell her that she shall conceive a child and call His name Jesus. Mary responded to the angel with such a great attitude, saying, "Let it be unto me according to your word."

What I love so much about this is that she was busy living her life when her life got interrupted. She didn't whine or complain although she was afraid at first. When the angel told her she had found favor, I realized that sometimes we are afraid of what is going on in our life but we, too, have found favor with the Lord. I saw her response and it amazed me because in Mary's time if you were pregnant out of wedlock (even though she had not known a man) you were judged and considered dirty. Yet, she still had joy. We go through things and we get so negative and complain. I looked at Mary's life being interrupted and realized that my life had been interrupted, too. How was I going to respond? I have always asked God to use my life for His glory so others will see Him in me, but how am I going to respond when I am faced with giants and would rather turn around and run?

Mary's example spoke volumes to me. I wanted to learn from her response, *let it be unto me according to your word*. She did not turn and run. She did not fight. She was scared at first but listened. She did not ask *why me?* She was willing to walk the journey set before her with a good attitude although she had some tough days ahead of her. I wanted to learn from Mary. My life was interrupted and I had no idea what was ahead of me. Not just the struggles, but also the victories. We are never a failure if we don't quit. Struggles are inevitable, but failure is optional.

PAM ESPINOSA

Chapter 4

ONE DAY AT A TIME

"For I know the plans I have for you,"
declare the Lord,
"plans to prosper you and not to harm you,
plans to give you hope and a future."
Jeremiah 29:11

Friday, October 23, 2009

I met my oncologist. I did not think I would ever have to step foot into an oncology office for myself, nor did I want to do it on this particular day. I approached this whole "oncology thing" with the idea that I would not need chemotherapy. After all, I already had my breasts removed, so I should be all done with this journey. To my shock and dismay, my oncologist told me that I would need six rounds of chemotherapy intravenously every three weeks. I would also have to take Herceptin because I was Her2 triple positive every three weeks for twelve months, and take Tamoxifen every day for five years. I could not do any reconstruction until I completed my treatment.

I would take Carboplatin.   Trade name: *Paraplatin.* *Carboplatin is an anti-cancer drug ("antineoplastic" or* "cytotoxic") chemotherapy drug. Carboplatin is classified as an "alkylating agent." It is used to treat ovarian cancer. Carboplatin is also used for other types of cancer, including lung, head and neck, endometrial, esophageal, bladder, breast, and cervical; central nervous system or germ cell tumors; osteogenic sarcoma; and as a preparation for a stem cell or bone marrow transplant. Carboplatin is given usually by infusion into a vein (intravenous, IV). *Source: chemocare.com

I also would be given Docetaxel. Trade name: *Taxotere*. *Docetaxel is an anti-cancer (antineoplastic" or "cytotoxic") chemotherapy drug. This medication is classified as a "plant alkaloid," a "taxane" and an "antimicrotubule agent." It is approved in treatment for breast cancer, non-small cell lung cancer, advanced stomach cancer, head and neck cancer and metastatic (spread) prostate cancer. Also being investigated to treat small cell lung cancer, ovarian, bladder, and pancreatic cancers, soft tissue sarcoma and melanoma. Docetaxel is given through a vein (intravenously, IV).* *Source: chemocare.com

Also I would be given Herceptin. Trade name: *Trastuzumab. Herceptin is a monoclonal antibody. This is used to treat metastatic (spread) breast cancer. It is effective against tumors that over-express the HER2/neu protein. As part of chemotherapy regimen for adjuvant treatment of lymph-node positive, HER2/neu protein positive breast cancer. It is not known whether or not this medicine may be effective in other cancers that may also have this HER-2/neu protein, including ovarian, stomach, colon, endometrial, lung, bladder, prostate, and salivary gland tumors. Trastuzumab is given through an infusion into vein (intravenously, IV).* *Source: chemocare.com

Tamoxifen: *an antineoplastic drug that blocks the estrogen receptors on cancer cells, used in the treatment of breast cancer.*

I appeared to be very strong while my oncologist spoke of my treatments. I felt so speechless, really. I was shocked that I would even need treatment. My husband felt just as speechless. After my appointment with my oncologist, the nurse walked my husband and I over to the treatment center, which would soon become a new reality for me. When I walked into that room I looked around and saw cancer patients with bald heads, hooked up to their IV's, reclining in their chairs, covered with blankets and sleeping. I felt a sudden rush of emotion overtake me. I was now officially a cancer patient and I could not hold my composure any longer. As I stood there crying, one of the nurses approached me and gently and lovingly shared with me that this would be a safe place and we would all become family. I could hardly hear her word's, much less process them, as the tears would not stop flowing. *Why me, Lord? I just don't think I can do this journey any more. I cannot handle this emotion.*

We left the doctor's office that day feeling numb, which made for a very emotional weekend; I felt so fragile, crying so easily. I had faith that as I entered this journey of chemotherapy I would have no symptoms or side effects from the treatment, and I would be as strong as ever. I knew God would carry me through this season because greater is He who is in me than he that is in the world (1 John 4:4). If God is for me then who can be against me (Romans 8:31)? I *know* I am healed. God is great and there is no one else like Him.

Family and friends came over and we all prayed together.

As they surrounded us, I could see we were becoming stronger. Stronger in our faith. Stronger in facing chemotherapy. Stronger in our love for one another as a family. They encouraged my husband and me, speaking the Word of God over us. By the end of our time together I was so encouraged and ready for my journey. God places the most amazing people in your life for such a time as this. I am so blessed. I will keep my boxing gloves on and stay in the fight. Times when my arms were hanging down I knew I had plenty of family and friends around me who would lift my arms up. These amazing people God has in my life have been so loving, so gracious, and so strong. Psalm 118:17: *"I shall not die, but live, and declare the works of the Lord."*

Friday, November 13, 2009

I started chemotherapy. I had fear in my heart now. I began to pray God's Word over myself – Jeremiah 29:11: *"For I know the plans that I have for you, declares the Lord, plans for good and not evil, to give you a future and a hope."* I asked God to give me courage and boldness to walk this season joyfully, that others would see Jesus in me. I prayed that all of this would not be in vain, but rather an encouragement to others that were going through difficulties. I also asked God to please let me keep my hair! *I already lost my boobs; can I at least keep my hair?!* My dad came with Michael and I on my first day. I had such a nervous tummy. I couldn't stay out of the restroom. I would come out and my husband would say, "Let's go," and I would run back to the restroom again. We prayed together and finally walked out the door, off to the unknown and nervous as crazy to face it.

As it turned out, I was unable to have treatment that day. We were told it was too late in the day to begin due to the time it took in the oncologist's waiting room and the length of time chemotherapy takes. I would have to come back on Monday, November 16. The nurse sat us down and explained the process of chemotherapy and the possible side-effects. Listening to this beautiful nurse was so overwhelming. My husband had a very hard time listening and came across as abrasive towards the nurse because he would ask questions and not like the answers. It made me nervous for him. I couldn't imagine what it must be like hearing all of this information concerning your spouse and the fear that you would have.

I was amazed at what God was sharing with me. He reminded me of how much I love my own children and that I would do anything in my own strength to protect them, provide for them, and cover them. Yet, He loves me in a way that is so much deeper than I could ever love my own children. He is God. He is covering me, protecting me, and providing for me. I am limited in what I can do, but He is limitless and can do anything. So why should I, in my own fear and doubt, limit God? I am amazed at God's everlasting and unconditional love.

My family and friends got together and set up a schedule of delivering meals to our home during the weeks I had chemotherapy. I was overwhelmed by their kindness and love for my family and I. They had already brought dinner after my surgeries so how could they possibly want to continue to bring dinners for us on this long journey ahead? I struggled with the idea at first, knowing that people don't have a lot of time or desire to make dinner for their own family, let alone mine, and I did not want to be a burden to anyone. My friends are truly amazing. Selfless. Loving. Kind. I had to get over myself and my pride and let others into my life to take care of me. I needed them. I wanted them. Having them take care of my family and me was another reflection of God's love and faithfulness toward us.

Chapter 5

UNCHARTERED TERRITORIES

"I will not die but live,
and will proclaim what the Lord has done."
Psalm 118:17

Monday, November 16, 2009

This day came very quickly. I got up and got ready to go to my first treatment. My dad arrived at our house early to go with my husband and me. It was so hard to leave my house to make the first step toward treatment. I would pray for peace and then run back to the restroom. At one point my husband said to me that if we don't get there and start the treatment then we will never get done with the treatment. Of course, it all makes sense to me, and I was fully aware of that; however, it was still so hard to take that first official step. I was reminding myself of God's Word – Proverbs 3:5-6: *"Trust in the Lord with all your heart and lean not on your own understanding. In all your ways acknowledge Him, and He shall direct your paths."*

We finally arrived at my oncology appointment. *The nerves!* I felt nauseated just being there. *Running to the restroom again. Here it goes. In through your nose and out through your mouth. Just breathe.* Between the fear and the anxiety, God began to calm me down. I began to have the attitude of, "Let's get this show on the road! I am ready to fight!" Truthfully, I am already victorious because of who I am in Christ; I needed to remind myself of this.

Although the nurse had previously explained to me what to expect, I still didn't know what to expect. They were amazing nurses - very friendly, speaking slowly and clearly. However, my mind was so busy trying to process the information there was no way to remember everything. They sat me in a chair to get my IV going. *Got my vein on the second try, not too bad.* Once the chemo started flowing I started feeling really light-headed. It scared me. The nurse stayed beside me to be sure I was alright and explained what was going on. Evidently it was Benadryl that was making me light-headed. They gave me so much Benadryl that the joke became I was drunk on Benadryl! As I sat there fighting to keep my eyes open, I asked the Lord to not let this journey be in vain, but to give me others that I could share His love with. That I could develop friendships and that others would see Jesus in me, even if it was just a smile as we all sat here in our recliners, hooked up to our IV, walking out our journey. I never did allow myself to go to sleep that first day of treatment. Truth be told, I was afraid to go to sleep. I wanted to watch everyone and everything, even though my eyes were crossing and I could not form my words very well.

After five hours of treatment I was able to go home. I felt fine other than being tired. I slept well until around 2:45 a.m. when I woke up and felt flushed. When I got out of bed in the morning I felt so shaky. I ate a little breakfast, which did help a bit. My husband stayed with me that day and it felt so good not to feel as yucky as I thought I would. I was rejoicing and thanking God for how I felt and prayed to feel this good after each treatment.

On Wednesday morning at 6:00 a.m., I awoke to the worst feeling ever. I felt so sick and so scared. I was shaking so badly and my body felt as though I had been ran over by a diesel truck. I really felt as though I was dying that morning. The sickness came out of nowhere while I was asleep. *I don't want to feel this way. I don't like it and it scares me.* I would not let my husband get out of bed. He had to go to work, but I did not want him to leave me. He prayed with me and held me in his arms. I felt so comforted and yet so scared. *What is happening to my body? This is only my first treatment, am I able to withstand more treatments? Oh God, I need your strength and your peace and your comfort.* Psalm 118:17: *"I shall not die but live, and will proclaim what the Lord has done."*

My mom came to stay with me while my husband went to work. His heart was torn in a million pieces to have to leave me, yet he knew I would be taken care of. Who better than my mom to stay and take care of me, her own daughter? I had nausea, the shakes, sores in my mouth, and could not eat for the next few days. My mom tried to get me to eat half a bagel and it took me 45 minutes to eat it. I knew I needed to eat, but I couldn't bring myself to get the food down. Between the nausea, the bad taste in my mouth that just would not go away, and my body aching all over, all I wanted to do was curl up in a ball and stay there until I felt better again. I felt bad for about three days until finally, a new day. I woke up feeling better! *Thank you Jesus for healing me! Thank you Jesus for your strength in the midst of my weakness.*

A week after my first chemo treatment I was feeling pretty good. I was extremely tired, however. I was excited to go to church. I knew I could not afford to catch any germs from anyone, but I knew I needed to be in the house of God. There is so much joy and peace being in the presence of others and worshipping God together. I went to church with a mask over my mouth and did not shake anyone's hand. We went out to lunch and it felt so good to be out! If every treatment can be like this then I've got it made!

Thursday, November 26, 2009

Thanksgiving Day. I have always been the one to host Thanksgiving at my home. I always have a full house and love it. This Thanksgiving was very different than what we were accustomed to. I had a hard time in the morning, feeling down knowing that things would be different. Then God blessed us! We were surprised by our friends who supplied us with a full Thanksgiving meal for our entire family. It was amazing! We felt showered with God's goodness and love for us. I put my mask on as we loaded up the food and went to my son and daughter-in-law's house and celebrated together. It was so beautiful! We went around the table and shared what we were thankful for. Going through an illness makes you realize what is really important and the blessings in your life: family, love, friends, laughter, health, God!

I noticed earlier in the day that I broke out with a full body rash. We had to go to urgent care that evening to get the rash checked out. They did blood work and, praise God, my white blood cells were not too low, which could have been the reason for the rash. I got a prescription and some Benadryl and was on my way. *Thank you God for your favor.*

Sunday, November 29, 2009

I was in the shower getting ready for church and as I began to wash my hair, I was literally devastated to get a handful of hair. My hair was officially falling out! I cried and cried and cried. I could not believe that this was happening to me. I was at a loss for words. I did not want to go to church. I did not want people to notice I was losing my hair. My husband convinced me that no one would be able to notice so we still went to church. I could only talk to God and tell Him that all I wanted was to be able to keep my hair, even if it thinned. I just didn't want to go bald. I was believing this would not happen to me. I couldn't seem to shake the feeling of devastation. I was freaking out.

I noticed a few days before that my hair looked "dull," like it lost its shine, but I never thought it was because it was about to fall out. *Please God, let me keep my hair!* I did not wash my hair anymore after that day because I did not want my hair to fall out quickly. I did not want it to fall out at all, so I certainly did not want to expedite the process!

After church my husband, youngest daughter, and I went shopping for wigs. This was very emotional for all three of us. My husband reminded me that God knew this was going to happen, it had passed through His hand first, and I needed to trust God. God really is my refuge, my strong tower, my strength, and my joy. I needed His joy to fill me again. I needed His

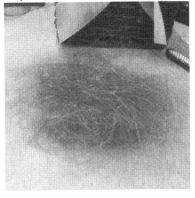

strength to rise in me again. Without challenges there are no victories! I love my Jesus! I did not find a wig that day. However, a few days later a friend and I went looking for a wig again. We laughed so hard trying on wigs and trying to get the courage to purchase one different than my normal hair style. As it ended up, I chose a wig very similar to my hair color and style. I did not want people to know that I lost my hair.

Wednesday, December 2, 2009

This was the day I was going to be fitted for my prosthesis. I was so excited for this appointment. Although I was adjusting to not having breasts, it would be nice to have some I could put on when I would go out of the house. I had a camisole that had little breasts built into it and that had become my favorite piece of clothing.

Trying on prostheses was a very different experience. The room was small and had boxes full of different sizes of prosthetic breasts. It looked like you were in a room full of shoe boxes, only when you opened the box there were breasts. It really was quite funny! I would try on a bra with a prosthesis and check to see if it was the right size for my body. We could not stop laughing! After many laughs we settled on a good size for me. Then we went back to the wig place to pick up my wig now that it had come in. It was so pretty. How comforting it felt to know I now had hair and boobs! I came home and immediately put my hair and boobs on and did it ever feel good! But, I just wasn't sure if I could get used to the idea of wearing a wig. *This will take some adjusting to, that's for sure.*

Chapter 6

EXPOSED

Friday, December 4, 2009

Tonight was Girl's Night Out, a women's conference at our church. I knew it wasn't a good idea being in a large crowd with the possibility of germs, but I craved fellowship with godly women. My pastor let me sit in her lounge and watch everything from there. It was an amazing time. The guest speaker that night was Cheryl Salem who herself had gone through cancer a few times. She has an amazing testimony and it was beautiful to chat with her for a little bit, and hear what God had done in her life.

That night, I wore my wig for the very first time. It was hard to not feel self-conscious about wearing a wig. Unaccustomed to wearing a wig, my head became very sore. I also got a hot flash and  wanted to rip it right off my head. Even though my circumstances were very different, I left church that night fulfilled and happy that I made the choice to go. *God is in control. He is forever faithful! I know I am healed and my heart jumps with joy!*

My oldest daughter, Kristin, called me today. She just broke down and cried. This was so hard for her. She didn't like to see me struggle and did not want me to do chemotherapy because the effects are so hard. My daughter lives a couple hours away and although she calls me daily it broke her heart that she couldn't be near me every day. I am just grateful to hear her voice; I know she loves me very much.

My youngest daughter, Kehlie, didn't say a lot but was always there with a hug. She offered me her hats to wear if I wanted to. She does not like to share her emotions, but I knew how hard it was for her to come home and see her mom lying down, not able to eat and going bald. She would come home and call out for me wanting to hear my voice to know I was okay. I saw that her heart was breaking. I saw it in her eyes as she tried to act like everything was alright.

My son, Michael, is pretty quiet. He is an amazing, sweet, and godly young man. He called me almost every day to check on me, give me scriptures, and pray with me. He always had an encouraging word. My daughter-in-law, Krista, was always so encouraging to me, as well. She was always smiling and willing to help. My son and his wife had the challenge of explaining to their children that Grammy will be okay.

It was very challenging for me not be around my grandbabies as much as I was used to. I missed my grandbabies so much and they missed their grammy, as well. We didn't want to take a chance of me getting sick; it was very important for me to stay as strong as possible. I went to their house wearing a mask, but it wasn't the same. They colored pictures for me and I hung them on my bedroom wall so I can see them from the bed. These kids knew how to make Grammy smile! How they warmed my heart! I knew God would redeem the time we had lost and would restore it back to us. That is how God is – He restores and He redeems.

I love how my kids are all so different and unique. God has placed each and every one of them in my life and they bless me incredibly. I could not have done this journey without such an amazing family who held my hand every day and walked with me whether they were near or far.

I was shocked by how much hair I was losing. I heard my mom whisper to my husband and daughter about the bald spots on my head. I was in such denial. I couldn't see the bald spots in the back of my head so it was easy to pretend it wasn't really happening. However, I saw the bald spots in the front and realized that my hairline was receding. I had not washed my hair at all since November 29. I knew if I did, I would get another handful of hair and I simply couldn't handle that. *Oh God, why is this hair thing so incredibly hard for me to handle?*

Chapter 7

INHALE, EXHALE

---

*"Cast all your anxiety on Him
because He cares for you."*
1 Peter 5:7

Monday, December 7, 2009

My second chemotherapy treatment. I was so nervous to go to my oncology appointment and the treatment center because I now knew what to expect. I could literally smell the chemo meds in my head and that alone made me feel sick. *Here we go again.* My mom came over to go with us to treatment. Once again she would stay the week with me. She is always such an encourager. You could see how much she enjoyed taking care of me. I prayed that this round of treatment would be less severe than the last one. I somehow felt stronger. As much as I was nervous, I also felt strength. *I can do all things through Christ who strengthens me!*

We met with my oncologist, who is such a nice, genuine man. He is so good at his job; you could just see how much he enjoys what he does. I could see in his eyes how much he genuinely cares for his patients. My blood pressure was pretty high that day – nerves, I am sure. I asked my oncologist if he suspected I would lose all my hair. He asked me to remove my hat and he pulled some of my hair, which of course I could not feel. He got a handful of hair and tells me, "Yep, you will be losing all your hair. It will be out within the next week or two!" I thought it was so funny the way he responded, but the news felt quite devastating. He also explained to me that losing my hair meant that the medicine was working for me. *Oh God help me to adjust and accept where I am. I know I need to embrace where I am in order to go forward.*

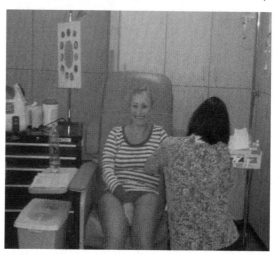

My lab results were great. God is always so good. I believe He is holding my hand, walking with me on this journey. I love God with everything in me and praise Him every day. *Now off to the treatment center – here we go again. Deep breath.* 1 Peter 5:7: *"Cast all your anxiety on Him because He cares for you."*

I sat in the treatment center on my recliner hooked up to my IV, once again trying to keep my eyes open, feeling fine but very emotional. I began to look around the room and pray for the people that I now had so much in common with. I prayed that they would know Jesus personally. I prayed that they would receive their healing. I prayed that

I would be able to smile at them and make a difference in their day. God adores these people. I wanted to just love on them. *Lord, help me to show your love to others today no matter what the circumstances are.*

I was feeling down on day three of my second treatment. I knew it was important to take care of myself, but I was feeling so nauseous I couldn't eat anything. *But, I am thankful for the rain.* My amazing husband was out Christmas shopping (which he loves to do) and even though I was happy he was doing so, it was very hard for me to be home alone. I was tired of not going out and being stuck at home. I was tired of feeling yucky. I was tired of feeling tired. The struggle was very real – especially the struggle with losing my hair. I knew it was only for a season, but I didn't want this season!

My friends wanted to shave their head to help me, but I asked them not to. I didn't want to see myself with a shaved head, let alone them. However, my sister chose to shave her head. I realized it made her feel good because she felt like she was supporting me, and I wouldn't take that away from her. I kept thinking how easy it must be to offer to shave your head and how hard it is to know you are going to *have* to shave your head. I had hair falling out everywhere. I feel like a dog that was shedding, but I still didn't have the courage to shave my head. I know it's just hair, but it's *my* hair. *I really have to get over this. Oh Jesus, how I need you. You are my strength, my joy, my healer, my everything! Encourage me. I love you.*

Chapter 8

MY HAIR
I Don't Know How To Do This!

"I can do all things through
Christ which strengthens me."
Philippians 4:13

Monday, December 14, 2009

Wow, what a day. I was home alone, which was very rare. Between my surgeries and chemotherapy, my husband usually had someone with me while he was at work. My mom normally would stay for five days after treatment. This day I was so happy to be alone and spend time talking with God. However, I began to feel jittery and shaky. I was not able to get in the shower. I could hardly breathe. I suddenly felt very anxious and fearful to be alone. I called my friend and she came to pick me up so I could hang out with her at her house. I was really trying to push through with my emotions, but I felt so emotional. *Why am I feeling such anxiety? Why can I not even take a shower?*

Once again I felt very emotional about my hair. Every morning when I woke up I would touch my head to be sure

I still had hair left. It was just weighing on me. As I sat at my friend's house, wrapped up in her blanket, I saw nothing but hair all over the blanket. I was at a loss for words. I text my hairdresser, who is a good friend of mine, to see if she would come to my house and shave my head. *Why do I have to do this? Why can't I keep my hair?*

That evening my hairdresser and her mom came to my house to shave my head. I just lost it and could not stop bawling! I was emotionally spent. I didn't think I could even go through with it and was afraid I wasted her time. Her mom, who I have known for years, said something very profound to me. She asked me why I was letting my hair have such control over me. I had not thought of it that way until now.

We all sat there as my hairdresser began to shave my head. As she was shaving my head, my head got so cold! I felt so vulnerable, just so strange, but I knew one thing: I wouldn't leave hair everywhere I went, shedding like a dog. It was such a defeating feeling when I left hair everywhere. I asked my hair stylist to leave a bandana wrapped around my head because I could not bear to even peek at my bald head, yet.

My head felt so cold. I needed to get used to the idea of being bald. I was not fond of the idea. This was really one of the hardest things I've had to do. I was very thankful for an amazing family and great friends who encouraged me and stayed beside me through the toughest of times. Boy, did I need God's amazing grace, His amazing peace, and His comfort! His mercy is new every day and tomorrow is a new day.

The truth is the following few days I fell into a deep depression. I didn't want anyone to see me. I didn't even want to see myself. I had to sleep with a beanie on my head at night because my head was so cold. I felt so vulnerable and depressed that all I could do was cry. *Why couldn't I have kept my hair?* Now, I felt like an official cancer patient and I did not like that feeling. People could look at me and know that I was "sick". *Oh God, please help me. Please encourage me and help me to get my eyes off of myself.*

After a few days of feeling this way (and not liking any moment of it) I woke up one morning and heard God tell me, "Get up. What are you doing giving the enemy such control over you?" I sat right up out of bed. *What am I doing allowing the enemy to play these games with me?* I decided it was time to take authority over my mind and my emotions. *I will not be ruled by my emotions or what my body looks like.* I prayed and spoke God's Word over myself. He was the one who said He would never leave me nor forsake me. I am a child of God. He said He goes before me and He covers and protects me. *I won't allow the enemy a place in my life. I will not allow depression.* I went to the restroom and stood in front of the mirror and told God, "Here it goes, it's just you and me," and took off my beanie so I could look at my bald head. As I stood in front of the mirror I laughed so hard I cried; I looked like a turtle, a little head and a big body!

I took a shower after that and washed my hair, I mean my head, for the first time in a couple of weeks. It was so strange to wash a bald head that belonged to me. My head felt so cold. I was officially bald on my head, arms, legs, eyebrows, eyelashes, and pubic area and I found this to be incredibly funny! Once again I asked the Lord to please use all that I am going through to help others. I just did not want what I was going through to be in vain. There must be a bigger reason why I am traveling this journey. I wanted God to be glorified in all of this. God is so good to me. He reminded me that He is always with me. He doesn't take us around tribulations, but He, hand-in-hand, will walk us through every situation. Doesn't it sound just like us to always want the easy way out? We want to be victorious, but we don't want to walk out the journey. I was glad to have the joy of the Lord in me for the joy of the Lord is my strength! He is always faithful. He does not ever leave us nor forsake us. He strengthens us, gives us grace for the day, one day at a time. *Oh God, continue to put a song in my heart and a dance to my step.*

Faith dispels fear and doubt. I had to push through and not allow the enemy to keep me down any longer. I had to encourage myself. I thought of how desperate the woman in the Bible with the issue of blood truly was. Matthew 9:20-22: *"A woman which was diseased with an issue of blood 12 years, came behind Him and touched the hem of his garment; for she said within herself, if I may but touch the hem of His garment, I shall be whole. But Jesus turned him about, and when he saw her, He said, 'Daughter, be of good comfort, thy faith hath made thee whole.' And the woman was made whole from that hour."*

I love how Jesus called her daughter. What a sweet and kind way to address her. Oh, how He loves us! I could really appreciate how desperate she was to receive her healing. She tried all the doctors of her day and she was still bleeding for 12 years. She must have been exhausted! Tired. I pictured a mass of people surrounding Jesus and she pushes her way through, crawling on her hands and knees on a dirt road, to touch the hem of His garment. He felt virtue leave Him and He said, "Who touched me?" His disciples thought He was crazy – everyone was pushing Him and He asked such a question. Jesus turns and sees this woman, whom He addresses as daughter, and tells her that her faith has made her whole. Wow! She had such determination. She was desperate. Have you ever felt this way, so desperate for a touch from God? *God, please, please deliver me.* I felt that desperate. I just wanted a touch from God Himself. Then, I realized that He *has* delivered me. He *has* healed me. He is the same miracle-working God yesterday, today, and tomorrow. We are a seedbed for miracles. He was walking with me, hand-in-hand, through it all. He also calls me daughter. I am His and He is mine. What greater love is there than this? Herein lays my peace and my comfort for my every day.

Chapter 9

I HAVE NO CONTROL – *BUT GOD DOES!*

"We are hard pressed on every side,
but not crushed; perplexed, but not in despair."
2 Corinthians 4:8

Monday, December 28, 2009

My third chemo treatment. My nerves were not as bad today. I was so grateful to have my husband and my mom with me. I loved the support I had. Today I wore my wig. I didn't want anyone to see my bald head. It made me feel good to wear my wig because I felt like I looked more like *me*. We got to my oncologist's office and received good news, my blood pressure was totally normal! My lab reports were all good. I felt so encouraged. It only took one poke to hook me up to my IV, which was wonderful (less poking!). It did not take long until I was very tired. The Benadryl they gave me made it nearly impossible to stay awake, but I was so determined not to fall asleep.

As I was reclining in my chair, one of my nurses was speaking to another patient. She came to me and told me the patient wanted to know if I had a wig on. I told the nurse to tell her the truth. The patient and I started chatting and I took off my wig to show her that it is not too hard to take on and off. We started laughing. This was very liberating because I went in with the idea that no one would see my bald head but now here I was, willingly exposing it for all to see. I had been asking God to lead me to others to share His love, so I was very happy to be communicating with this beautiful young lady. As it would end up she was only a couple years younger than me. Her name was June. We quickly became friends as we shared our stories with one another. I left treatment feeling pretty excited to have found a new friend. Although tired, I physically felt good.

I heard from others how encouraged they were watching me walk out this journey; they said I was so amazing. Truth is I am not so amazing. It is God who is so amazing, showing Himself through me. It is all Him. He is so faithful. His love, His peace, and His grace are so overwhelming. I looked forward to completing my treatment and having all of this behind me, but for now this is where I am. I knew He would never leave me but strengthen me consistently.

I was sick again. The chemo got harder every time. It wears on you. I felt that the first two days were okay but by the third day, I got so nauseous I couldn't get out of bed. I couldn't eat and every smell was horrific. I felt like I was pregnant again, but worse. I constantly got asked how I was. Well, truth be told, I felt horrible. I wanted to cry. I wanted to hide in a dark room and not talk to anyone. I was gassy from the chemo and that hurt, too. I had sores on my gums. I was feeling very anxious. My heart fluttered and I felt out of breath. I made a conscious decision that I was not going to complain. I will respond with *tomorrow will be a better day*. I knew it would be better than today because it can only get better. If tomorrow is not better then that is okay. I will continue to say *tomorrow will be a better day*. That better day will eventually come.

God will continue to strengthen me. He gives me a song in my heart. God is so amazing. He meets you right where you are. Before I even opened my eyes I could hear a beautiful song inside my heart. *I am the Lord that healeth thee, I am the Lord your healer*. I opened my eyes ready to leap with joy. I could see how much God loved me. I fall more in love with Him every day.

I began to feel a little discouraged with how my body looked. I mean, being bald and having no boobs is not exactly appealing. I struggled with the idea that my husband had to come home to me looking like this every day, and I felt like I was not able to satisfy his needs. He works all day and comes home to having to take care of me. I wanted to take care of him.

I missed my life as it was before I got sick. I realized how much I used to complain about my hair and now I would love to just *have* hair. I used to complain about my breasts being too big, but now I would just love to *have* breasts. I am struggling and the struggle is real.

I was about to take a nice hot bath and stood in front of my mirror, naked, just looking at myself. I was disappointed with what was looking back at me. I felt like me, but I sure did not look like me. Suddenly (and God is a God of "suddenlys"), I heard God whisper to my heart and tell me that I am not identified by what the mirror says.

I am not identified by my hair or my breasts. I am identified by who He says I am. He says I am victorious! He says I am redeemed! He says I am restored! He says I am delivered and I am whole! He says He is the lover of my soul! I am so in love with Him. I rejoice in who He is. I feel like I am riding on the very wings of His grace!

Something very funny happened today. I went to the grocery store to pick up a few items and to enjoy being out of the house. When I came home I walked through our laundry room and my wig got caught on a clothes hanger that was hanging and the wig came right off my head as I kept walking. It was the funniest thing! I laughed so hard and thanked God for the joy that He shares with me.

Monday, January 18, 2010

My fourth chemo treatment. My husband, mom, and I were off to see the oncologist once again. Great news, my platelets are high, my white and red cell counts are high, my blood pressure is normal, and my immune system is not too low. I am doing so well! Off to treatment again. I was so happy to see my friend, June.

We made sure we sat next to each other so we could chat. We were so funny – we would talk but the Benadryl would kick in for both of us so we would stop mid-sentence and not remember what we were saying. We would just laugh at ourselves and say that we were drunk on Benadryl. We "got" each other.

Once, I had to use the restroom and could hardly walk. My husband had to literally hold my hand and walk with me; we laughed so hard!

I found that this treatment was harder to bounce back from and to regain my strength than the last one. I was so thankful for my family and friends who came and helped me. My routine became when I had chemotherapy my mom stayed the week with us, usually about five days. By the weekend I was usually feeling better, just very tired. I was happy to be able to go to church on Sunday, be in the house of God, and hear an incredible word from our pastors. I am so blessed! The week following treatment I felt much better, only tired. By the third week I felt a lot better, but then it was time for treatment again.

I had friends that came and spent the day with me. They fixed me lunch and then we would watch a movie. However, the joke was that I always fell asleep during the movie! My friends all pitched in and hired a cleaning lady to clean my house; that was huge for me! I am such a clean freak, so not being able to do what I wanted to do was challenging. I was able to run to the grocery store and maybe get a little lunch (and I was so happy to do that), and then I would come home to nap.

I had the nerve to run to the dry cleaners' with only a hat and no wig, and I was so blessed to meet a beautiful young lady who recently went through breast cancer herself. I was so encouraged to hear her story. God is good like that – He will put people in your life just at the right time. A divine appointment. I felt like God was sharing with me that it was okay and I would be just fine. I left the dry cleaners' crying, just so touched by God.

Chapter 10

SEASONS

Saturday,
January 30, 2010

I was having an emotional day again. Sometimes it's so hard to keep pushing through. I felt so unattractive. I didn't feel sexy in any kind of way for my husband, who is the most amazing, loving, caring, and thoughtful man! He went to every single treatment with me. He's taken such great care of me; he's selfless, always putting his own needs and thoughts aside. I wanted to lie in bed and feel his strong arms around me and just stay there; I felt so safe in that space.

We have been together since we were 18 and 19 years old. We had no idea when we got married at that young age that we would face so many battles together – the biggest one being my cancer. There is no way to know where you will be in 20 years, but I have learned that together and with God we can fight anything. We are an amazing team. We really do complete each other. God paired us together before we were in our mothers' wombs.

We are such opposites. We met at McDonald's where we both worked. He would always ask me out and I would say no. He was not my type. I was very quiet and shy, a good Christian girl. I was very sheltered in a lot of ways. He was not a Christian. He was very loud and outspoken. He was far from sheltered. I finally told him I would go out with him, that way the next time he asked I would be able to say I didn't think it would work out. On our first date I picked him up and took him to church to see a Christian music group called Sweet Comfort Band. He smelled like marijuana (I was pretty disappointed in that), but we had a great time.

My parents were pastors of a local church. Michael would come to church with us every week. At first, it was to "score points" with my parents, but soon the word of God grew in his heart and he loved coming to church. He accepted Christ and began to grow in the things of the Lord. Before we knew it we were together every day and fell madly in love with one another. However, we were not perfect by any means. I got pregnant before we were married. Although my dream was to get married and have children I did not expect to start so young. We knew we wanted to get married and spoke of it often, but we were planning on waiting a few years. We got married a month after we found out we were having a baby. Our sweet married life began on October 3, 1981. Never have I looked back and had any regrets. God knew exactly what I needed in a husband long before I ever did.

We had a beautiful baby girl, Kristin, born in May of 1982. I laugh now remembering how she survived me being a first-time mommy and not knowing what to do. She is an incredibly bubbly, loving, caring girl, touching and changing lives everywhere she goes with that beautiful smile and laugh. Kristin is a gorgeous girl inside and out.

We were blessed again in May of 1984 with a handsome baby boy, my son, Michael Jr. He was such an incredible little guy. He was always so quiet. People questioned whether he knew how to talk. He did talk, but he had an older sister who loved to do all the talking for him! He was always so gentle and so loving. To this day my son touches and changes lives everywhere he goes. You don't have a conversation with this amazing young man without walking away thinking he has wisdom beyond his years and is one great looking guy!

Four years later, in June of 1988, we were blessed again with a beautiful baby girl, Kehlie. She truly made our family complete. She was her brother's and sister's "baby." She was a joyful child, always giggling and always smiling. Everyone loved to play with her; she was so easy-going and fun. She is still a very fun young lady, very caring and giving in so many ways. She lights up a room with that gorgeous smile of hers. Kehlie is gorgeous inside and out.

We are so richly blessed to have three amazing and beautiful grandbabies in our family, Haydin, Noah, and Morgan. We have another grandbaby on the way as I write this.

At this point in my journey I was really looking forward to being done with this season of breast cancer. I wanted to be done and have a new and joy-filled season of life. I wanted to go to church freely, without a mask, and be able to hug people and shake their hand without having to use hand sanitizer right afterwards. I wanted to be around my grandbabies without a care in the world. I wanted to be able to be involved at church again and be a part of other peoples' lives. I wanted to not be so tired. I was ready to move on. I knew God's grace would continue to see me through. I rejoice always that God is so good to me and I am healed and whole. Tomorrow will be a better day.

Thursday, February 4, 2010

I went to see the doctor for a bad cold, but they couldn't give me anything for it. *I know I am healed by the very name of Jesus.* My daughter-in-law, Krista, and my grandbabies came to hang out with me and I couldn't have been happier. Krista is the sweetest of sweets. She is so loving and caring. I am so blessed that she enjoys spending time with me and brings her beautiful babies. Those little ones just make me laugh. This was the first time I let my grandbabies see me without a wig. They had no idea I was bald.

I was in the kitchen with Krista and the kids were playing in the other room when I decided to take my wig off. Haydin, my oldest granddaughter came in and said, "You're so pretty, Grammy." Noah, my grandson, walked in and said, "Put your hair back on, Grammy!" Morgan, my youngest granddaughter who was only 20 months old at the time, would just stare at me and smile. She would rub my bald head; she loved the feeling of it. All three children had different reactions. We laughed so hard!

Chapter 11

TOMORROW WILL BE A BETTER DAY

---

*"It is good to praise the Lord and make music to
your name, O Most High, proclaiming your love
in the morning and your faithfulness at night."*
Psalm 92:1-2

Monday, February 8, 2010

My fifth chemo treatment. My mom was unable to come
with me because she was sick. I was so sad. I loved having
her there with me. Every time she had to leave my house
the week after treatment I just cried. I am so thankful for
her. I am so thankful she is gentle. There is nothing like a
mama's love. She would lie down next to me on the bed,
rub my head, and just be there. I know she was so
saddened to not be with me that time.

My husband and I went to meet with the oncologist. My
counts were a little low. He wasn't sure if he wanted to
give me treatment. I silently prayed. I wanted to stay on
track with the treatments. *I know I can do another
treatment today, God is my source.* My oncologist decided
to go ahead with treatment.   When I walked in the
treatment center I saw my friend June. I was so happy to

have her to chat with and be drunk on Benadryl with while we had our treatments. I also loved when my children and friends came by and visited me while I had treatment. The people at the treatment center were becoming like family. I had the best nurses ever. I could see being friends with them outside of the treatment center. I think you have to be a pretty special person to be an oncology nurse. It must be so hard to always be so encouraging when you are working with cancer patients, but these nurses were extraordinary. I never looked forward to the treatment itself, but I did look forward to seeing my beautiful June and my beautiful nurses.

I was so tired and so nauseous a few days after my chemo treatment. Chemo is so hard on your body. The more chemotherapy treatments you have, the harder it becomes for your body to bounce back. My immune system was so weak. I was really struggling with gaining strength and building my energy. However, I continued to see the beauty and grace of God through it all. I knew tomorrow would be a better day. I praised God that I only had one more of these tough chemo treatments left. I believed that God would use everything I had gone through for His glory. God says He will never leave me nor forsake me. I am so incredibly thankful!

I love experiencing God's faithfulness. Before I even opened my eyes in the morning I heard a song in my spirit: *"For You are great, you do miracles so great, there is no one else like You."* It made me so joyful to hear those words inside my spirit. I realized that God speaks to me, sings over me, and rejoices over me, and it has nothing to do with me but everything to do with Him! I am righteous through Him. I am healed through Him. I am experiencing

His grace like I never knew was possible. Zephaniah 3:17 has become one of my favorite scriptures: *"The Lord your God in your midst, the mighty one, will save; He will rejoice over you with gladness, He will quiet you with His love, He will rejoice over you with singing."* My spirit is always rejoicing and praising Him. He literally takes my breath away! Challenges are inevitable; defeat is optional! You are never defeated if you don't quit. Don't ever give up!

I was so blessed to have a friend come over and take me to lunch. It was so nice to share all that God was doing in the midst of feeling so overwhelmed with this journey. All I could think was nothing could compare to the Name of Jesus. It made me think of that song that says, *"When you don't know what else to say, say the Name of Jesus."* There really is no other name above the name of Jesus. Psalm 92:1-2: *"It is good to give thanks to the Lord, and to sing praises to Your Name, O Most High, to declare your loving kindness in the morning, and your faithfulness every night."*

Monday, March 1, 2010

My sixth chemo treatment. I was so glad that this was my last! I serve an amazing God. He has brought me this far and has always kept His word to me. I was trusting God for great reports when I saw my oncologist. I knew this was my last chemo treatment, but I would still need to continue treatment every three weeks until November 2010 for Herceptin. This place really had become my family. Treatment every three weeks for a solid 12 months is a very long time.

My numbers were good enough to get treatment started. I was amazed at how emotional I felt. I couldn't believe that I was actually going to be done with this part of my journey! Some days it seemed as though this day would never come, and now it was here! Of course, I was so excited that after this my hair could start growing back (Herceptin doesn't cause hair loss).

Well, like I said previously, the more chemotherapy you have the harder it is to bounce back and regain strength. I was really struggling. I felt such anxiety. My heart was beating so fast I could hardly breathe. It was hard to feel so weak, to smell food and become nauseous, and, even worse, trying to eat! I was so tired of feeling so yucky. I had to keep reminding myself that this was the last one and I could make it through. *I am an over-comer! Tomorrow will be a better day!* I needed to stay in bed, meditate on God's Word and His faithfulness. I needed to remind myself that He is made strong in my weakness and that His grace is sufficient for me. I was reminded of Psalm 25:5: *"Lead me in Your truth and teach me, for You are the God of my salvation, on You I will wait all day."* I was literally am waiting on Him. *I know He hears me. I know He is my source of strength and that He carries me when I can't stand up. I know that this too shall pass and I am so grateful for that!*

There was a special guest at church and I really wanted to hear him so I pulled myself together and went. It was so challenging for me. The Word was great to hear (the Word of God is always great), but I really struggled with anxiety. My heart just wouldn't slow down enough so I could breathe. I had such bad hot flashes that I wanted out of my own skin. *There are too many people here. I have nowhere to run.* I tried to be calm. Once, a person stopped me to ask how I was doing and I lost it. I felt like ripping my wig off my head and running out! I was finally able to get away from the crowd, the questions, and just breathe. *Time to go home and go to bed.* I had no idea how draining that would be for me. I couldn't get out of bed for three days. I was amazed at how broken I felt. *Oh, how I need God.*

PAM ESPINOSA

Chapter 12

STAY AMAZED

"I remain confident of this: I will see the goodness of the Lord in the land of the living.
Wait for the Lord; be strong and take heart and wait for the Lord."
Psalm 27:13-14

I thank God for a new day and that my days are getting better. I am beginning to feel stronger. Through Him I can do all things. I thank God for His message He drops into my heart. He tells me I am victorious, I am joyful (His joy is our strength), I am more than a conqueror, I am healed, I am saved, I am free! I am free to worship Him, I am free to love Him, and I am free to serve Him every day!

Monday, March 22, 2010

I had my first Herceptin treatment. I loved the fact that it was not so time-consuming. My other treatments were around four hours, but my Herceptin was done within an hour and without side effects. It sure was nice not to leave so exhausted and not to get sick. God is so good! I did not see June at treatment that day. I prayed for her; I just love her. She had such a beautiful smile and such a beautiful spirit about her.

I had to go to the hospital and meet with the oncologist/radiologist and got great news – I do not need radiation! I was jumping for joy! I believed God that I would not need radiation and it was amazing to hear that good news! I listened calmly while the doctor was talking, but when we left his office I could not stop the tears! Praise God! I am moving onward and upward.

Monday, May 3, 2010

I turned 48 years old today. I was so blessed to celebrate another year. An experience like this makes you put things into perspective. I love the family that God so generously blessed me with. He is so good to me! I had my oncology appointment today. I prayed and asked God for great results and my oncologist told me my blood work looked great, just like I prayed! My white blood cell count was increasing. From my last appointment (three weeks prior) it improved from 2.7 to 4.4! I loved how faithful God has been to me. It made me think of the scripture, Psalm 27:13-14: *"I would have lost heart, unless I had believed that I would see the goodness of the Lord. Wait on the Lord; be of good courage, and He shall strengthen your heart. Wait, I say, on the Lord."*

I was beginning to see my hair growing back in. Wow! I am so excited to see little hairs growing in! I was so happy about this! Of course, I still needed to wear a wig or a hair wrap but it felt good to see hair. It came in pretty gray. I read an amazing book earlier in my journey called <u>Any Day with Hair Is a Good Hair Day</u> and I loved it. It is a good day to see hair on my head! I laugh now at how hard of a time I had about losing my hair.

I received an email from my friend, June, from the treatment center. She was feeling down. She got results from her PET scan that showed no positive results in her cancer shrinking. My heart broke. I love June and I loved having the opportunity walk this journey with her. I prayed for my sweet, sweet June. I knew God is more than able and He is all we need, but when I hear reports like that it brings me down. Then a little bit of that old familiar fear creeps into the back of my mind and I have to conquer that fear with the Word of God. 1 John 4:18: *"Perfect love casts out fear."* I always think of fear as F-false E-evidence A-appearing R-real.

Saturday, May 22, 2010

I was officially introduced to the Relay for Life events. One Day. One Life. One Community. My husband, children, grandchildren, and I participated. It was amazing and so beautiful. I did the survivor walk with many other women who fought a similar battle as mine; it was so empowering. I loved being with these amazing women. My family stood on the sidelines cheering me on. All I could think was, "Really God? Really? This is too amazing!" After the survivor walk, my family and I did a few laps together. It felt powerful and so incredibly emotional. After a few hours we all left and had breakfast. I love my family! I truly have the best family ever!

This day also was one of the most amazing days of my life. I shared a vision with my family and close friends that was burning in my heart. I wanted to gather everyone together that helped my family and me throughout this process and celebrate them with food and a time of thanksgiving. I wanted to bless them. Instead, they all blessed me. My family and close friends made this vision come to pass more beautifully than I ever expected. My dear friend opened her home for our victory celebration. We invited my whole family and all our amazing friends. We were blessed with approximately 150 people who came and shared this day with us.

My husband and I were able to share with everyone how much they had blessed us. We gave praise to God for all He has done. We had our friend, who is a pastor, blow the shofar as we all had a victory shout and released pink balloons into the heavens. The sky was amazingly beautiful. The moment was breath-taking, emotions were high, and the presence of God was tangible. I am so very blessed. I felt so loved by God and every family member and friend that is in my life. God is so good to me! I will forever sing of His praises daily!

Thursday, May 27, 2010

My pastor asked me to speak at Girlfriends Bible study group. I was excited to share my story thus far. I have never been much of a public speaker, but I wanted to shout from the mountaintops what God had done in my heart and in my life. God is more than enough and more than able to use my life for His glory. I was reminded of a scripture I confessed when I first got diagnosed, Psalm 118:17: *"I shall not die, but live, and declare the works of* the Lord." I did not die, only to myself and my own ways. I am living and now declaring the works of the Lord. I wanted others to see that they can choose to trust God in all areas of their life. I wanted to show others that there was hope for whatever situation they were facing. It was so beautiful to share all that He had done in me and through me.

While I was sharing at Girlfriends I took a big step and took off my wig and publicly showed my bald head. Although I had a few hairs growing in, I was still basically bald. That was so liberating for me. I believe we need to be real with people – no masks. We need to show others that we have struggles, too and that we have a God who is in love with us. He gave His life for us because of His unconditional and undying love. I think we are in the practice of acting as if everything is okay when we are really crying out for someone to just listen. If we can start being real with our struggles and our victories others will not feel alone. Their barriers will come down and we can love each other with the love of Christ. I don't ever want to forget all that He has done for me and in me. I am forever grateful to God.

I had another treatment on May 28. I trusted God that the nurses would find my vein on the first poke because getting poked over and over again as your veins begin to roll is very hard (it really does hurt). It would bring tears to my eyes and then I would feel bad for my nurses because we were all friends now. That is what happens when treatment becomes your life every three weeks for (now) seven months. I began to get very excited to be done with treatment and start the reconstruction process. Although I must say, being able to just "put boobs on" when I want has become a way of life for me. Many days I don't even

arms. I needed to build my muscles and get better mobility in my arms. I was also attending Pilates and yoga classes and could feel myself getting stronger. The gym had a drawing and I put my name in and was so blessed to win a free massage! I am highly favored!

My hair was coming in pretty well. It was so curly. My husband colored it for me. I thought if I dyed it then it would give it some depth. What I got instead was a very burgundy red head! My family laughed and I cried! I ran down and got some color corrector which worked well to remove the color out of my hair! Next time, I will wait until I have enough hair to go to my hairdresser and color it correctly! I reminded myself how blessed I was to have hair again and not to complain.

I was blessed to go to lunch and the movies with my beautiful friend, June, and her husband, Jay. I loved being with her because we related so well with where we were in our lives. It was hard to hear that she was not receiving good reports from her oncologist. Her cancer was not shrinking. She wondered if she should even continue with her treatments. This was her third round of cancer and she was getting exhausted of always fighting. I prayed for her daily. I loved to see her and her husband laughing together and enjoying each other. We are not promised tomorrow. What if we lived each day like it was our last? What if we enjoyed the presence of those we love every day and not waste time on focusing on the non-essentials?

I was so happy to be asked to preach at a women's conference at church. I was so excited and so nervous. I trusted if God opened this door for me then he would equip me. It was not about me but about Him who dwells within me. Like I said previously, I have never been much of a public speaker but I love to share the love of God wherever I go. I love to share all that He has done. His Word will never return void and I can trust in that.

It was now the end of July, 2010. I was getting closer to completing my Herceptin treatments. Once again my oncologist said my counts were looking great and the nurse got my IV on the first try. God is faithful! Yes, even in the small things! Nothing is too big and nothing is too small. God cares about every detail of our lives. What moves our heart also moves His.

I felt so blessed to be able to go to church without a mask now and to be able to hug people freely. I love being in the presence of God; it truly is the most fulfilling place to be. Whether at church or at home, God is with me and I feel Him and His peace. I pray He shows me how to love others the way He loves me. I pray He shows me how to show grace to others the way He has shown grace to me. I pray He shows me how to forgive others the way He has forgiven me. I don't live my life unto myself but unto Him. I want to live my life in a way that others don't see me, but they see Jesus.

I went swimming today. I wondered how I could wear a swimsuit without having breasts. To remedy this problem, I decided to sew foam pads into my swimsuit. They make swimsuits with "boobs" but I didn't own one so I took matters into my own hands! It was fun to make and it made me realize that even though I had gone through a lot, I can always find joy in the journey. Every day is a blessing. We can become better or we can become bitter.

Moving day arrived. We found a beautiful home to move into. Of course, it was sad to leave our home, but it was exciting to see what was ahead. New beginnings are always a little challenging, but it is a good thing. Change forces us to get out of ourselves and embrace where we are so we can move forward.

I began meeting with different doctors for consultations on reconstruction. I was getting closer to completing treatments and starting the reconstruction process. It was amazing to hear all the different opinions. You need wisdom to make the right choice for you. I just wanted to look and feel "normal" again. I knew it would be a long process and had no idea what I was getting myself into at this stage of the journey. I had no doubt that God would lead me to the right doctor and I would have peace with whatever decisions were made. I was grateful that I was already having consultations so I could have a clear mind and clarity about what was ahead of me.

Chapter 14

THE MORE I SEEK YOU

Monday, August 30, 2010

Today was a sad, sad day. I received a phone call from my friend, June. June and her husband had been visiting her parents out-of-state and there was a bad accident that took the lives of both her father and her husband. I was devastated and in shock for her. *Why God? Why? I simply don't understand!* My heart ached for her. I didn't know what to say. June was shocked, hurt, disappointed, and scared. She said she was supposed to be the one to die first, not her husband. She also told me she decided to stop her chemo treatments. I was so devastated. I could understand in some small way why she wanted to stop treatment. She felt as though she had no reason to keep going through these tough treatments when her body was not responding to them. She wanted to have some quality of life as she lived her last days. I couldn't stop crying at the thought of us not doing our treatments together, at the thought of her leaving life here as we know it. I love June so much. I love that God brought her into my life. My heart hurt as she hurt. I remember when my husband performed her wedding ceremony and the laughs we had. Now he will perform the memorial services for her father and her husband. *How do we do this Lord? It is so devastating. God, you are our strength and our place of refuge.*

89

I had another oncology appointment before treatment. I was praising God for His faithfulness. My numbers were good! I only had two more treatments to go! I was getting closer to being done. Soon after, I had a consultation for reconstruction. It made me excited for what was ahead. God is so good to me. He fills me with His joy. I literally felt as though I could feel His arms around me, holding me and comforting me. I had a song in my heart by Kari Jobe called "The More I Seek You." The lyrics are beautiful. They described my heart and how God made me feel so complete in Him.

"The more I seek you, the more I find you
The more I find you, the more I love you
I want to sit at your feet,
drink from the cup in your hand.
Lay back against you and breathe,
feel your heart beat.
This love is so deep; it's more than I can stand.
I melt in your peace, it's overwhelming."

Thursday, October 7, 2010

It had been one year since my granddaughter, Haydin, had surgery for her kidney. Haydin was only 18 months old when doctors discovered what was ailing her. She would continuously cry and we couldn't figure out why. She was admitted to the hospital for a week while they ran tests and found that she had a kidney infection. Barely 24 hours after Haydin was released from the hospital she was in incredible pain. She got sent to a different hospital where they admitted her. Haydin was there for a full week before being released. They found that her ureter tube (tube that carries urine from the kidney to the bladder) was twisted, but they wanted to see if it would get better and straighten out on its own. However, it got worse over time. Haydin had to go through a lot of tests. When she was five years old they decided to operate.

I found it incredible that between my surgeries my beautiful grandbaby would also be having surgery. It was good for Haydin to see her grammy have surgery first because then she felt like she could do it, too. Haydin was on a gurney ready for surgery and wanted the shield of faith that she had drawn. She knew God would protect her. She was such a brave soul. She wasn't crying; she had an amazing peace that came from God alone. This little, beautiful granddaughter of mine went through so much pain before and after surgery with an amazing attitude. Although she would cry because of the pain, she always said she knew God was with her. She encouraged me in ways she could never understand. God is always so faithful, even when we don't understand why things happen the way they do. God has a perfect plan.

I was amazed at how fast time seemed to be going. I had completed the necessary consultations for my breast reconstruction and chose a plastic surgeon I felt comfortable with. I was very excited for the next stage of this journey. There are different options for reconstruction and it is hard to know which one is best. I looked at all the options and prayed and discussed with my husband which one would be best for me. I didn't look forward to having surgery, but I was ready to begin this stage of my journey. I didn't have any tissue on my chest, just a little bit of skin. I found out that as my skin stretched over time with the expanders I may be able to be a size C cup. I was just happy to have breasts at all!

Chapter 15

EMOTIONAL DAZE

For we live by faith, not by sight."
2 Corinthians 5:7

Monday, November 8, 2010

It was my last day of treatment. I had such mixed emotions. I was happy to complete these treatments but I would miss the friends that I made here. The nurses were some of the sweetest people. They always made me laugh. They were amazing. The fact that this place had

become so familiar to me (it had been a big part of my life these past 12 months) made this a very emotional day.

93

I celebrate and honor the people that show up every week for their treatments regardless of how they feel. They are not moved by their feelings. That is not easy. I am sure they, like me, wanted to turn around and run the first time they stepped foot in the treatment center. I saw them without hair, wrapped up in their blankets, some sleeping, some reading, some smiling, and some looking defeated. I wanted to hug them all because I understood how they felt. I now understand that this treatment center in some ways defines them, but not like you'd think. I believe it defines them as being strong, as being brave, and as being courageous. I believe they are amazing people. Their smiles light up a room because they know how to be grateful for each day. They don't take life for granted because they have faced life and death straight on. We all have our battles. We have all had the horrible thought *what if someone tells me I have cancer?* Yes, that is scary to hear, but the truth is we are not defined by cancer. It is only a word – it is not a death sentence. Although cancer has taken many lives it does not mean it will take mine or yours.

After I completed my last treatment we went to dinner to celebrate with my family and nurses. These nurses, let me tell you, are an amazing group of women. I truly believe that it takes a special person to be an oncology nurse. They come into their place of employment every day knowing they face life and death firsthand. They come in with a smile on their face, a love for the people who are there, and such compassion and determination to help these patients beat cancer. They hold your hand and encourage you. They become a loving friend and tell you they are with you every step of the way, and they mean it. They become your family. They remind me of God. Let me tell you why. They knew my name. I felt loved and valuable. God knows you and me by name. God loves you and me with a personal love. God considers you and me highly valuable. He adores us. No matter what you have believed in the past, believe this one truth: you are perfectly loved by God.

Thanksgiving was here! I was thrilled that this Thanksgiving I could bless my family and make our meal. I am blessed and thankful every day, but this day was special because the year before I was unable to prepare our Thanksgiving meal the way I normally would have. I was done with treatment and thankful for what was ahead. I was excited to see how things would unfold as I approached the next stage of this journey. I faced it with joy and excitement. I saw all that God had already done and was ready to see what was next. Life is not so bad when you know who holds your tomorrow and your today. Hand-in-hand with the lover of my soul!

My friend, June, was amazing. I loved visiting her every week. Her mom lived with her and helped her. June had such a sweet spirit. Her smile lit up the room and I loved listening to her laugh. I loved our heart-to-heart conversations. She was getting weaker but had such determination. She began slowly packing her belongings and dividing them among her kids and grandkids. June insisted on giving her car to my son. She wanted to bless someone who had kids and needed a car. I really struggled with receiving this but was very grateful. She signed the pink slip and made me promise to give the car to bless my son and his family, which I joyfully did. To this day I am so blessed every time I see them in that car. I smile from ear-to-ear and shed a few tears. June was one of the most generous and loving gems I know. I loved that through this journey I was blessed to become such good friends with her. She was a warrior. She showed such strength at a time I would want to run. She looked death in its face and it didn't paralyze her. Instead, she walked through gracefully. I had asked her how she wanted me to pray for her and she kindly told me, "Pray that the transition is easy for me." That was one of the hardest things I had to do. I honored her, and therefore prayed daily that she would transition into heaven smoothly, without pain, and be embraced by her family that she loved so dearly.

Chapter 16

UNDER CONSTRUCTION

---

*"I can do all things through Christ
who strengthens me."
Philippians 4:13*

Thursday, December 2, 2010

My husband and I decided to celebrate the end of treatment by going to New York. Neither of us had been before. It was so beautiful in New York that time of year – beautiful holiday decorations, the hustle and bustle, walking around Central Park, and restaurants. What we did not plan on was me being so exhausted. I had a hard time walking for too long. I constantly needed to return to our hotel room to rest. We enjoyed every day, but we say we need a "do-over" where we can fully enjoy the beautiful city without the interruptions of running back to the hotel room to nap! I am just happy to be alive. I am happy to have a husband who loves me and enjoys spending time with me. I am happy that we are able to travel. I am blessed! I am honored to live my life with God, my husband, my family, and friends. I don't ever want to forget what I have gone through or take anything or anyone for granted.

We had such a beautiful Christmas. It was so special to me

that I had the strength to go Christmas shopping. It is such a joy to give gifts to your loved ones. As I was purchasing gifts for my family members I was reminded that the biggest gift we could give is ourselves. Our love, attention, kindness, compassion, empathy, laugher, smiles, and hugs are priceless. Take time to enjoy each other. Don't judge one another or let small annoyances begin to grow; it's just is not worth it. Have a listening ear and an open heart towards one another. Greet each other with a hug and a kiss. Family is an amazing gift. We have been given the greatest gift, Jesus Himself. How can we not give the best of ourselves to those we love? I try to live this way, not only toward my family but to those I come in contact with. Why not try to make a difference in someone else's life? It may not be someone I know, but my act of generosity can change their moment or their day. Just a thought.

I met with my plastic surgeon to begin reconstruction. I was on my way to rebuilding all that was taken physically. This beautiful surgeon was recommended to me by a dear friend of mine and she really does amazing work. I was so impressed with her. She came into the room and read my pathology report and knew what breast size I previously was just by reading how much tissue was removed. Now, that's a good surgeon in my book!

Thursday, January 20, 2011

Today was the day for my first reconstructive surgery. They put expanders in and filled them with a little bit of saline solution to get my skin to begin to stretch. It's been a year and four months without breasts. This was exciting and a little nerve-wracking. I woke up four times in the middle of the night with this word running through my mind: *fight the fight, run the race, finish the course with joy.* I felt so amazed at God and His faithfulness to me. He amazes me. He strengthens me. It reminds me of 2 Samuel 22:40: *"You have armed me with strength for the battle."* I really can do all things through Christ who strengthens me (Philippians 4:13). My surgeon was amazing. She is a believer as well and prayed with me before surgery. It was such a comfort knowing that my surgeon trusts God. The power of prayer!

The surgery was quite painful, just like my surgeon said it would be. At one point after surgery I hadn't even opened my eyes yet and felt excruciating pain. As painful as it was I was still so blessed. It was amazing how good I already looked with the expanders and 250cc of saline. It felt so amazing to be where I was now in this journey. Sometimes it felt like I would never get there, thinking it was just so far away, but now that I was there it seemed like it had gone fast. God is so good. I honestly can say I love Jesus more than life itself. He amazes me. He sweeps me off my feet like a true love can only do. I want my heart and my life to be an expression of His heart and His love for us.

Wednesday, February 16, 2011

This was my first "fill up." I was so nervous; I just did not want to experience any more pain and did not know what to expect. The process was not like I had thought. It was the strangest thing. The surgeon used a magnet that was on the end of a long string and swung it in front of my breasts until the magnet connected to the expander, which allowed them to know where to inject the saline. It did not hurt to inject the saline; it only hurt once it was full. She injected 100cc in my left breast and 150cc in my right. My right breast appeared smaller than my left because the cavity on my right breast was deeper than the left. This process was very uncomfortable for three days. I was growing boobies! It reminded me of a funny thing my granddaughter, Haydin, asked me one day. She knew I didn't have breasts and asked me, "Grammy, are you growing breasts again?" Oh my goodness, my heart melted. I love the innocence, sincere hearts, and honesty of children.

Chapter 17

JUNIE BUG

"As iron sharpens iron,
so one person sharpens another."
Proverbs 27:17

Friday, February 18, 2011

I got a call from June's mom saying we needed to come over to see her. This was so very hard. We walked in the room and hardly recognized her. It broke my heart. I know that the last thing to go when a person is passing away is their hearing, so I wanted to talk as normally as I could to her. I told her how much I loved her. I told her to go see

her husband, her dad, and Jesus. His arms are wide, ready to embrace her. I could see her lips moving and I was sure she was telling me she loved me, too. I told her that when it is my turn to go home to Heaven I wanted her to be at those front gates welcoming me alongside Jesus. I leaned in and gave her a hug and a kiss.

Leaving her that day was a tough thing to do. I knew that was my last time to see her until I spend eternity with her. The very next day, February 19, 2011, I got a call from June's mom saying that she had passed away. June is now with Jesus every day. It's amazing how as my heart breaks, I also rejoice. I rejoice because she is no longer in pain. I rejoice because I was blessed to become friends with such an amazing person. My heart breaks because I can no longer see her, hug her, or talk with her. I long to see June again one day in the sweet by-and-by. *Thank You, Lord, for my beautiful Junie Bug and how she touched my life in such a special way.*

Chapter 18

BE OF GOOD CHEER

---

*"Wait on the Lord; Be of good cheer,
and He shall strengthen your heart;
Wait, I say, on the Lord."*
Proverbs 27:14

I was getting "fill-ups" every three weeks. The more my skin stretched, the more it hurt. I had to take Vicodin to help with the pain. I usually have a high tolerance for pain, but these fill-ups really hurt.

Now that my fill-ups were completed, I had to wait three to six months before the next surgery to replace the expanders with implants. While I waited my skin would continue to stretch and relax. I was so happy that I still had a few months before my next surgery.

Wow, God is amazing! He continually puts people in my path to share what He is doing in and through my life. I never would have chosen this battle, but I have no regrets and am blessed that God would use someone like me to share His love, goodness, and kindness with others. I have met so many women that are on their breast cancer journey. It may be a different type of breast cancer than mine, but fighting the battle and knowing you are already victorious is a battle in and of itself.

Proverbs 27:14:
"Wait on the Lord; Be of good cheer,
and He shall strengthen your heart;
Wait, I say, on the Lord."

My implant surgery was a few days away and I was excited and nervous at the same time. I didn't like the idea of surgery, but I loved the idea of completing this journey. I went in for another check-up for my "growing" breasts because my right side looked smaller than my left. My doctor had to do another fill-up. It appeared my expander had a leak. I was grateful this would be my last fill-up; they really hurt!

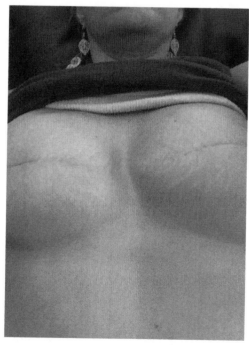

Thursday, September 1, 2011

Surgery Day. Implant Day. I was so excited. They took me back less than five minutes after I arrived and had me prepped for surgery within an hour. It went so fast that I don't even remember them taking me in to the operating room.

My husband said I was awake and talking, but I have no remembrance of that at all. They must have given me some good meds! This surgery was not nearly as painful as past surgeries. My skin was already stretched. The right breast was a little more painful because of the issue with the expander leaking and the skin on that side not being as stretched as the skin on the left side. I was so very grateful that this surgery was complete.

I am blessed beyond words for my family. Once again, like every other surgery, my husband and daughter slept in the living room with me. They prepared my medicine in Dixie cups with the time written on them, all ready for when I needed to take them. They were on a rotating scheduling to get up with me throughout the night to give me my medicine. This had been the process for every surgery. *I am so blessed!*

I looked so "normal" with a little hair growing in and new breasts. I was feeling pretty good. I was excited for my hair to officially be long enough to style. I am doing very well!

Chapter 19

BIG SURPRISES

Saturday, October 1, 2011

Michael and I went to Jamaica for our 30th wedding anniversary. I am so happy to celebrate life with my amazing husband. He lights up my world and always makes me smile. He takes such good care of me. He is a constant reminder of how much my Heavenly Father loves me. Michael loves to embrace me and shower me with his love. I take joy in all that God has blessed me with.

Our hard days are overshadowed by our great days. We all have seasons of hard times, but we also have seasons of great times. The key is to realize those hard seasons are temporary and time will bring

better and greater things. We need to realize that we are walking through the valley of the shadow of death but it is just that, a shadow. Shadows don't live – they only exist. We don't want to live like a shadow. If we get up and do only what we *have* to do, not thinking about the past or the future, and we only *exist* that is living like a shadow. God is our very strength. He is our encourager. He is the lifter of our heads. See, His love knows no limits to its endurance, no end to its trust, no fading of its hope; it can outlast anything. His love still stands when all else fails. God is love and He loves us unconditionally, even in our hard times. Hold on to the One who holds your today and your tomorrow. His grace is sufficient for you.

Saturday, October 15, 2011

I thought we were going to a friend's wedding today. I was in for a *big* surprise. My husband blindfolded me and drove me somewhere. I had no idea what he was up to. After he took off my blindfold I saw my two daughters and my hairdresser. We were at my church and they planned a ceremony for Michael and me to renew our wedding vows, which is something I always wanted to do. My daughters and hairdresser fixed my hair and my make-up and had a beautiful dress for me to wear.

Our actual wedding day was very simple, and it had always been a dream of mine to have a beautiful wedding with a fun reception. This is exactly what our kids planned for us. My dad performed the wedding just like he did on our actual wedding day. That was so special to me; I adore my dad!

Our daughters walked my husband to the altar. My son walked me down the aisle – talk about a "proud mom" moment! As my son was walking me down the aisle, and I beheld my handsome husband and my handsome daddy, I was overwhelmed with such love and joy. It was amazing to enjoy this moment with the ones I loved most. Seeing my daughters, my grandbabies, my mom, my family, and my friends overwhelmed me with joy that flooded my heart. My husband placed a brand new wedding ring on my finger! *Really?* I was in shock and couldn't stop crying. I felt so beautiful and so loved. After the ceremony they threw us an awesome reception. I still smile from ear-to-ear when I remember that beautiful day in my life.

They had a beautiful cake and an awesome D-Jay. To hear my kids make a toast to us... what else can I say other than, "Wow." These kids blew me away by their love and their generosity towards us. We had more fun than we did on our original wedding day! We had the best time laughing and dancing. Our kids also blessed us with a night away. These amazing kids of ours put so much work and thought into all that they did. I never could have imagined that they would do this for us. We are so blessed! I told you I have *amazing* kids!

Chapter 20

JOY COMES IN THE MORNING

"Weeping may stay for the night,
but rejoicing comes in the morning."
Psalm 30:5b

Thursday, November 17, 2011

My final surgery. The doctor performed nipple and areola reconstruction. I was excited to complete this transformation, but I also had a little anxiety. I was ready to be done with these surgeries. I was ready to move forward. They took skin from my lower abdomen to create the nipples and the areolas. As I sat in the waiting room I chatted with my husband and a couple friends to help keep my mind occupied until they called me back.

The doctor was amazing; she encouraged me and prayed with me after I was prepped for surgery. I felt more at peace. After surgery my pain did not feel too bad at first, but I had the shakes and was freezing and could not get warm. They gave me medicine that helped the shaking so I could feel calmer. My abdomen was sore where they took the skin, as well as the new nipples and areolas. However, I kept telling myself this was it and it would all be over soon. I am so blessed to have new breasts now. I felt like I would look "normal" once again. But more importantly than looking normal was the joy that I felt in my heart and the grace that I felt every day from my Heavenly Father. He loves me with a love so deep none can compare. His love is unending and unconditional, and His grace is sufficient always.

I was beginning to sleep better, even a little on my side. It had been two years since I slept on my side; no sleeping on my tummy, yet. My lab reports were all great. I am so blessed.

I had to have one more minor surgery in March, 2012. The nipple on one of my breasts would not "shrink" as it was supposed to and looked very odd. My doctor cut some of it so it would look more natural. It has healed up and looks wonderful. I continued to see my plastic surgeon as she monitored the healing process of reconstruction. I praise God that I decided to go through the complete reconstruction process. Although it has been a long road, it feels rewarding after all I went through while battling cancer.

My oncologist said they still consider me in active treatment so I am on a pill every day. I was taking Tamoxifen and am currently on Arimidex. However, I know I am cancer free and completely healed. Currently, I see my oncologist every six months and visit the treatment center often. Every October I take pink cupcakes for breast cancer awareness. I love my nurses and enjoy our dinners and conversations. They are amazing people that God strategically placed in my life for such a time as this. I always want to remember what I have experienced and what God has done in and through me. I count it all joy because this season of my life has made me stronger.

Nobody can take away what God has done inside of me. He took me from a place of brokenness to a place of healing, a place of complete trust and rest in Him. Although I never would have chosen this journey for my life, I am grateful to have gone through it because of my heart and my life being forever changed. I want nothing more than to show off my Jesus and all He has done. I *am* healed, I *am* whole, I *am* redeemed, I *am* an overcomer, I *am* victorious! I am all these things and more through Him who gave His all for me.

Remember, whatever you may currently be facing is not too big for God. He is more than enough. Challenges are inevitable; defeat is optional. Do not ever give up!

Chapter 21

MY BODY, HIS PAIN

*"This is now bone of my bones
and flesh of my flesh."
Genesis 2:23*

His fear and pain are often overlooked in the midst of her disease. This chapter is very important. You will hear my husband's perspective of this season in his life. Breast cancer doesn't affect only the woman. It also strongly impacts the man who loves her. In many ways, I think the experience is much harder for him, partly because he feels so powerless. My husband, like most men I know, is a "fixer." But this is something they cannot fix. What they can do is love you, pray for you, support you, and reassure you. Now for my husband's story.

*****

Written by: Michael Espinosa, husband.

I met Pam for the first time when I was 17 years old. I got to know her a few months later and realized I wanted to learn more about her as time went by.

I realized early on that she was not just a beautiful young teenager but something else. She was different in so many ways, which was not common or normal to me. I felt she was time-warped from the fifties and put into my life. Yes, *my* life!

I married Pam at the very young age of 18 and we committed to live life together to the very end. I would be there with her, for her, and by her. That vow and commitment has allowed us to experience life together with highs, lows, and everything in between. Let the exciting ride and journey begin!

September 11, 2001 was a day that would change my view of the essential versus non-essential things. Of course, I am speaking of the attack on the Twin Towers, which caused much loss, heartache, and pain to so many families.

Friday, September 11, 2009 was also a day that would impact my view of life. It was a day that changed my love and admiration for my wife, increased my faith in my awesome God, strengthened my walk with Jesus, my Lord and Savior, and solidified my position as a covering for my wife and adult children. The morning started with an early rising – getting ready for work, praying with Pam, and off to work. A few hours later, while at work, I received a phone call from Pam with some news that punched me square in the face and gut at the same time. I listened to Pam tell me what the report said, told her it was going to be alright, and that I would be home very soon. As I was driving home, I was so thankful I didn't have hundreds of thoughts going through my mind. My only thought was Jesus Christ, my Savior, who I had called on as a teenager, and how He would help me walk out and live what I had confessed, preached, and believed for nearly 30 years.

As I arrived home I was thinking of what my first thoughts, emotions, and words would be to Pam. In that moment all that mattered was seeing the look in her eyes and letting her know we were doing this together. I would do this with her – every second of every minute of every hour of every day. *Every day.* We hugged, cried, and prayed as we prepared to meet with the doctor later that afternoon. The results were not favorable and the doctor said surgery would be necessary. The question we had to answer was if Pam would have to have one surgery or multiple surgeries based on where the cancer was detected.

Over the next three weeks Pam had various tests performed: MRI, ultra sound, biopsy, lumpectomy, etc. I trusted God, but I also went into the mindset of "I'm going to fix it" as I realized this was going to be a fight. Taking it on myself and putting a plan in place, I found out pretty quickly my solution would crash and burn. I was reminded of something that took place in January of 2009. I was spending my time with God over the first few weeks, talking to Him about my dreams and goals for the New Year. I was quickened in my spirit and repeatedly kept getting this message: "It is a time of preparation, stripping, and pruning. Begin to prepare now." I told Pam I didn't have an explanation or understanding of that, but I knew God's voice and I knew I had to begin to step out in faith and prepare.

Over the course of the next eight months I experienced losing my job due to company bankruptcy, getting hired by a new company with a significant reduction in pay, losing our home, and getting news that my wife had cancer. Up to this point, I have touched on a few things to get you to the place that really touched and changed my life as the journey of caregiver became my life.

The months of preparation were beginning to have a purpose in so many ways. I began to understand that the preparation was to trust God, hear His voice, respond to His direction, have faith in Him, and be able to rest in Him.

Caregiver – a word that I never spoke, knew the definition of, or thought I would ever relate to. Take a look at the definition of these words:

- <u>Care</u>- Close attention, protection, responsibility, to look after
- <u>Giver</u> – Devote, sacrifice
- <u>Caregiver</u> – A person who helps another individual with his/her activities of daily living

Although I was described and recognized as Pam's primary

caregiver, I want to share with you the raw experience and reality of what it was like to walk in my shoes. My endless love, my friend, my lover, my wife, my Pamela was hit with such a force that it knocked her down and she had to reach for the ropes (God) in order to get back on her feet.

I asked God to show Himself real to me like never before. I needed to be whatever was required of me for Pam. I wanted her to see whatever she needed to see in me at that moment, any moment, and every moment. I would not be able to do this without the Holy Spirit moving in me and through me every day. One of the very first things I told Pam was that we had to be united in this fight and I needed her to be as blunt and honest with me every day regarding how she was feeling and thinking. I told her I would be sensitive and compassionate when I needed to be, otherwise, I would be a fighter winning every round of this battle.

The miraculous happened every day for me. I did not realize in the beginning how much my life would change and how it would shape the rest of my days. I was not Pam's caregiver per se; I am her husband in everything, every day. I dedicated and gave Pam all of my attention for over two years. I did this without hesitation and without so much as a break. Looking back, there were no pity parties or thoughts of "what about me" or "I have needs, too." There was nothing to detract or distract me. Consider this: I watched my wife have five surgeries, have her large, beautiful breasts removed, lose her gorgeous hair, and literally become bald from head-to-toe. She began chemotherapy treatments that caused her to become sick, tired, and anxious. She lost her appetite, which made eating a long process every day, causing her to lose approximately 25 pounds.

I woke up every two or three hours in the middle of the night to give her two to three types of medication, take her to the bathroom and literally clean up after her, help her shower, and get in and out of bed. When this was done, I went to work, always leaving someone with Pam. I would compartmentalize my thinking while doing my job (so productivity wouldn't drop) and then went home and repeated what I did in the morning. Kehlie, my daughter, was there to help in the evenings. Kehlie and I were pretty selective and very protective over Pam regarding visitors. There were times precious family and friends would come over and we would determine if they were turned away or could visit for a short time. We appreciated their love and support, however, Pam was the priority!

I would like to share some real experiences that were strictly between God and me that were painful to the core! It was pain that I had never come close to experiencing, greater than the loss of my parents or family members, or disappointment in my personal or professional life. Hebrews 4:16: *"Come boldly to the throne of grace that we may obtain mercy, and find grace to help in time of need."* I can say the pain I was having from seeing the constant, consistent, and relentless disease that Pam had to contend with every day made me feel defenseless. The close and intimate relationship that I was experiencing in a vertical way with God allowed me to express so many things to Him that no one else would ever be aware of or hear me speak. I would talk to God and cry out to Him in many ways – talking, yelling, pleading, petitioning, and crying until I couldn't cry anymore. He saw so many sides of me, and the greatest thing about it was

He spoke to and responded to me in any state or condition I was in.

Hebrews 4:15 tells us Christ sympathizes with our weakness and we can confidently approach the throne; we must know our prayers are welcomed. God's throne of grace shows us unconditional love, help, mercy, forgiveness, empowerment, and an outpouring of the Holy Spirit. You must know this: we can *always* seek the help we need. This personal revelation allowed me to walk this out in a way that seemed normal. What do I mean by this? I approached every day focused and determined to be whatever Pam needed or wanted me to be!

I can say my role as caregiver, aka, husband to my wife, was surreal, which is a way of saying this "supernatural" way of living became natural. Asking and seeing God truly, truly increase my capacity in so many areas was like seeing miracles manifested every day. A few examples:

- When I looked at Pam in her breast-less and bald state, I didn't look past it. I looked right at it and saw how much more beautiful she was inside and out – *really*!
- Personal and quality time that enriched our relationship and did not include going to the movies, dinner, or a weekend getaway. It meant caring for her, feeding her, holding her hand, giving her medication, bathing her, taking her to doctor appointments and chemo treatments to name a few. It brought us closer together.
- Learning how to be physically intimate and passionate with Pam in a new way increased my love and respect for her to an all-new high. This all

happened without having sexual intercourse for well over one year. Our physical intimacy prior to her illness was healthy, so the obvious thought is, "Yeah right, how was intimacy maintained?" The natural mind and human desires would say it's impossible. However, I was very fulfilled and the only way to describe this is supernatural!

- Security, protection, and covering everywhere, every day, all of the time. In the home or in public, at the grocery store, doctor's office, church, or running errands. Being the proverbial "bodyguard" gave me a personal sense of showing Pam how precious, valuable, and important she is to me. God is our protector.

- Believing God for the provision and seeing Pam being built up with so many things that mattered at that particular moment such as scarves, wigs, prostheses, hats, clothes, special dietary foods, and specific hygiene products.

The pain that I experienced watching my dearest Pamela Jean was so hard. The feeling I had of not doing enough, falling short and failing as her helpmate and husband was tough. Let me tell you how God pulled me out of that ugly situation – Pam. I'll explain it this way: through all of the adversity Pam had to go through she was the real-life, visual, and physical example of how awesome God is! Without recognizing or declaring any particular thing, she imitated our Savior Jesus to help, strengthen, encourage, pray for, and love people to life when the situation would seem like the opposite should happen. Pam, being the purest of the pure, took this and clearly defined who Jesus is in a powerful way rather than allowing cancer to define her!

Ephesians 5:22 speaks of the Fruits of the Spirit which are love, joy, peace, endurance, gentleness, goodness, faith, meekness, and self-control. I witnessed Pam bear all of these fruits every single day while walking through the fire. Many of us are challenged and may struggle doing one of these nine on any given day! This is what God used to lift the pain I felt as a husband and a man, and what motivated me and kept me focused on the end result — victory in Jesus!

I hope and pray you can receive the powerful, real, living truth of what I described — Jesus plus nothing! He has done it all, we don't need to add anything this side of the cross — Jesus plus nothing.

Pamela Jean, my hero, my love, my life, my wife!

Chapter 22

HEARTFELT TRUTHS FROM MY FAMILY

Our family is a circle of love. Our circle is strengthened with every challenge faced, every blessing celebrated, and every joy shared. Together, we are unbreakable. Family is forever.

When cancer hits you personally it affects the whole family. I felt it was important and necessary to have a place for my children and family members to express their experience during this journey. I believe it will encourage you as you read their beautiful stories. I know it was not easy for them to put into words. They are very real and raw while they expose their hearts with you.

*****

Written by: Kristin Espinosa, daughter

My mom is the most amazing woman I know. I have always had a remarkable amount of respect for my mom, but after watching her go through breast cancer, there is a level of admiration, respect, and love I have for her that I didn't know existed. Watching my mother go through breast cancer was scary, remarkable, torturing, and inspiring all in one breath.

My mom's cancer diagnosis came at a time when I hadn't

felt as close with my family as I had in years past. Getting this kind of news makes people pause and take inventory of those things and people who are most important in their life. This is definitely what happened. I felt time freeze. I had almost taken my mom for granted knowing that she was always there, just a phone call or a short drive away. Instantly, my mind went to - is my mom going to die? Of course, I didn't say this out loud, but I had never experienced that fear of possibly losing my mother. Our family all came together like never before and there was something very beautiful in that. Still, there is a bond there that this created that can't be broken. While I would never wish for a kid to watch their mom go through such a fight, I am grateful for what grew within our immediate family.

First was the removal of lymph-nodes and the lumpectomy, and the next thing I knew, she was getting a double mastectomy. It all happened so fast, I am not sure I had a real moment of clarity. Every time I would see my mom before and after surgery, she had a smile on her face. Her strength was fierce. It was a quiet confidence that she had within herself, and I am happy to see her use that voice in this book. I know her faith and her family kept her going. There are two things I can say for sure, my mom's faith is strong; it can't be shaken. Secondly, her family is everything. Nothing brings her more joy than all of us being together in one room.

I would call my mom every single day to check on her and see how she was feeling. Without fail, she would acknowledge that she wasn't feeling great that day, but she had hope that tomorrow would be a better day. I would call the next day and it was the same thing: "I am not feeling great today, but I'm sure tomorrow will be a better day." She never lost hope. I loved it. She kept believing tomorrow would be a better day until, eventually, today was better than the day before.

After my mom's double mastectomy, when she was going through chemo, was by far the hardest time to get through for me, for my mom, and for our family and friends. It felt like her chemotherapy treatments lasted an eternity. Slowly but surely I watched her get stripped of all of her outward signs of womanhood – her breasts had been removed, her hair was gone, her body was small and frail. It didn't resemble what I knew my mom to be. Sometimes I would call and get her voicemail to be greeted with, "Hi, you've reached the Espinosa's. We're not able to get to the phone right now…." her voice was full of pep and life, and it sounded like my mom. But when I would hear her voice on the other end of the phone it didn't sound like that anymore. The pep was gone. That was hard to reconcile. I wanted my mom back. I wanted her to never be sick again.

Slowly but surely she made it through. Chemo was over. She got stronger, her hair grew back, her body changed, she got that sparkle back in her eyes, and her voice was full of pep again. I am not sure I can ever really express what this was all like to watch and be a part of, but I know this story will carry on to bring hope to people who need it and understanding to those who feel alone. I am blessed beyond measure to have Pam Espinosa as my mother. She embodies unconditional love and acceptance. She's a person who will rejoice with you in your accomplishments and mourn with you in your times of sorrow.

My mom has redefined womanhood and beauty for me.

She has shown me the power of faith and hope. She continues to show me the impact of unconditional love. She is fierce and full of life, unafraid to be vulnerable and share her story. She's my biggest fan and I can't imagine the world without her.

*****

Written by: Kehlie Carpenter, daughter

I can remember the moment my mom was diagnosed with cancer as if it happened yesterday. On September 11, 2009, I was getting ready for work when my mom walked in my room. The tone in her voice told me the news before she even spoke the words: "I have cancer." We instantly held each other and cried together. I knew she was waiting on results from a biopsy and, of course, knew cancer was a possibility, but when it became the reality it was gut-wrenching. I remember that day feeling strong and at peace, saying, "It's okay Mom, we are going to kick cancer's butt!" However, as the diagnosis began to unfold and I watched my mom go through her journey fear began to creep in. At the time, I was the only child living at home with my parents so I was there day in and day out helping care for my mom. I remember when she had her first surgery, which was a lumpectomy, and sleeping on the couch with her, setting my alarm to wake up every three hours to make sure she was getting her pain medication. I took care of my mom, and I took care of her like she would have taken care of me.

Not long after her lumpectomy the second blow came finding out that her whole breast was infected and she would need a second surgery. I remember how hard it was knowing my mom was not only going to have a second surgery, but that she needed a double mastectomy. A double mastectomy made it even more real that my mom had breast cancer. It was hard for me to come to terms with that. When I was at home, normally my safe place, I felt I had to be strong for my mom. I felt I couldn't show any fear or cry because I didn't want her to see that in me. Plus, my mother, the one I would normally talk to when I was having a hard time, was the one who needed the support, not to be the support. Home really took on a whole different feeling; home was now where I went to be my mom's protector and caregiver, and to be my dad's support. My dad and I became a team in a whole new way. Being with my mom during her recovery from her double mastectomy was easy because there was nowhere else I would have wanted to be but right beside her (emptying her drains, helping her to the bathroom, feeding her, etc.). Still, being with my mom was so hard. I hated seeing my mom go through that. She was so strong and courageous, but it didn't make the fact of my mom fighting cancer any easier.

I remember the third blow when my mom told me her oncologist said she was going to need chemotherapy. That was probably the hardest thing for me. My mind went into a tailspin and I remember thinking, "Oh my gosh, is she going to lose her hair?" I don't know why, but that was so hard for me. I didn't want my mom to have chemotherapy, to be sick, to lose her hair, or to lose weight. I think all of those things really solidified that my mom was a cancer patient. With her double mastectomy she could wear prostheses and still look like my mom on the outside, but with chemo she was going to change.

Once her treatments began it didn't take long for the change to start happening, and of course my dad and I became way more protective with people because the last thing we wanted was for my mom to get sick. My mom's hair had officially started falling out. Not only was it getting everywhere, but she had a bald spot on the back of her head. This was one of the hardest parts for me. But, one of the hardest parts of the process actually brought the most laughs. The funniest things would happen when my mom would wear her wigs! Those laughs are what get you through and lift some of the heaviness. Some of my favorite and funniest stories to tell actually come from when my mom had cancer!

Watching my mom endure chemo, not only with the hair loss but also with feeling so sick in her body, was the most fearful time for me. I remember coming home every day and walking through the door and yelling, "Mom!" to listen for her response. I didn't even care if I woke her because if she responded then I knew I wasn't going to walk into a situation I was terrified of.

Eventually, chemo ended. My mom had reconstructive surgeries, her hair started growing back, and she was no longer amidst the battle but had overcome. However, sometimes I still deal with that same fear I felt in those moments and will forever be my mom's protector, making sure she doesn't exhaust herself or get too sick. There are still doctor appointments, blood draws, and daily pills that my mom deals with. Her journey still isn't over, but what she has done with her journey is beyond inspiring.

My mother is truly the strongest, most inspiring woman I know. She fought her battle and was able to help countless lives with her experience, encouragement, and faith. If I at my strongest am like my mother at her weakest then I would be proud. Her journey really became our journey, and when we were in the middle of it felt as if it was never going to end. It is truly mind-blowing to know we are through it and stronger than before. As much as I hated my mom going through breast cancer, I am so grateful for what it did in my life and how it changed me. Here is a verse that reminds me of my mom who fully relied on God to get her through and has allowed Him to take her battle and turn it into her victory song. Psalm 73:26: "My health may fail, and my spirit may grow weak, but God remains the strength of my heart; he is mine forever." When God remains the strength of our heart victory will be the outcome!

*****

Written by: Michael Espinosa, son

I remember my mom calling me at work, telling me the tests came back and the results were cancerous. I could hear in her voice she was shaken, but standing strong in her faith as she faced the unknown future that was now before her. The saying goes, "It's not what happens to you, but how you react that matters." Throughout the whole journey, from the beginning to today, she chose to walk in faith, speak life, and look to Jesus in the midst of it all trusting the outcome to Him (Romans 8:28). She used the pain and difficulties she faced as an opportunity for the Word of God to come alive in a new way. She held tightly to the promises of God for years and is now walking in the fullness of them. No matter the obstacle, life circumstance, or doctor's report my mom has shown me that Jesus is with me, He is for me, will strengthen me, and hold me through it all (Isaiah 41:10). She's an amazing mother and woman of God.

* * * * *

Written by: Krista Espinosa, daughter-in-law

I remember the day we all gathered together as a family and our parents shared the news that Pam had breast cancer. We cried together and we prayed together. We didn't really know what to expect but we knew God's Word and we were going to stand in faith for His promises, even if we couldn't see them in the natural.

It's amazing how one phone call can change your whole life. Life as we knew it was about to change into a season we had never personally been through. At that time, my children were five, three, and fourteen months old. Pam was a very active and involved grammy. I was a stay-at-home mom and could use all the support I could get! In a matter of days it went from Pam watching the kids or having the kids over for some grammy time, to many tests, surgeries, and chemotherapy. On top of this new season my oldest child Haydin, who was five, was getting ready for surgery on her kidneys a week after her grammy's first surgery (her lumpectomy). Needless to say, we were a family in prayer and fighting the good fight of faith!

Looking back, it brings tears to my eyes to see how God was so faithful in a season turned upside-down. He was our anchor holding us firmly in the storm. Seeing Pam walk this fight of faith was hard in the natural but beautiful in the spiritual. Watching a loved one go from being healthy and able to do practical things, to hardly having enough energy to get out of bed, was difficult. Pam went from having a busy schedule and always loving on people to her "new normal," which was doctor appointments, chemotherapy, and resting at home.

The beautiful thing was seeing her faith and love for the Lord not be shaken by the word "cancer." In fact, her love for the Lord and for people grew even stronger! She was so strong in the spirit even when her body was weak in the physical. Pam was the glue for her family and held us all together by her love and support. It was time to be there for her and do what she had taught us – to stand in faith and keep our eyes on Jesus.

Although I do not wish this upon any family, I'm grateful for the many things we learned as a family through this trial. We leaned on one another for support. We loved and encouraged each other. We were Team Mom! We were going to protect her. What the enemy meant for evil, God really turned around for good!

When we talk about all the memories of that season we laugh and cry. It really brought us closer as a family and closer to God. Going through this has taught me to never take our time together for granted. Always appreciate your everyday lives even when it seems monotonous. Appreciate the fact you get to wake up in the morning to go to work. Appreciate the fact you have an appetite to eat. Appreciate your health. Appreciate the fact that you have energy to spend time with your children and grandchildren. It's truly a blessing to have all these things we take for granted. These were just a few things my mother-in-law didn't have for a season.

Pam has taught me to allow God to walk us through the trial and to not stay in disappointment or fear. She has taught me to be fearless and that it's possible to have joy in a difficult season. Pam never complained or asked, "Why me?" She fought the good fight of faith and is preaching her testimony to everyone she comes in contact with, literally, even at the grocery store. She truly is an inspiration to everyone who knows her! I'm so proud to get to be a part of her life and in her family!

*****

Written by: Haydin Espinosa, granddaughter (11 years old)

Hi, I'm Haydin Espinosa and when my Grammy was going through cancer is was scary because I was having surgery and we all needed to be in faith. We keeped our hearts right and Jesus helped us. I was healed and my Grammy. Now we look back on those years and rejoice for all that is done with. While we were going this we read Proverbs 31:25: *"She is clothed with strength and dignity and she laughs without fear of the future."*

So whatever you're going through read this verse and trust in the Lord and He will help.

*****

Written by: Zelma Wyatt, mother

When I first learned that our daughter had breast cancer I was put into another realm of emotion. My mind was going in so many different directions. Of course, my heart immediately felt broken. Soon following, my mind and my heart took a different direction and I knew what my part was concerning my beautiful daughter and what she was facing.

Going back into memories of not too long ago, I began to think about the years when her dad and I lived in Idaho. I had become a caregiver. My responsibility was to go into the homes of wonderful people that needed care. This was the beginning of a journey I knew not of. Once a month, my place of employment would have a meeting. In those meetings we had teachings about taking care of those who couldn't take care of themselves completely. The principles that really hit home to me were always protecting those I cared for. Whatever they felt as independence for themselves, I was not to hold them back. The other principle was to always be positive with them. If there was anything going on in a negative sense, I was to build them up and give them a sense of confidence and usefulness. Encourage them.

I took these principles to heart for our daughter, Pami. When she began her chemo treatments, I was there with her and Michael, who we call our son. It was not just a few minutes of chemo but much longer. However, watching her keep a smile on her face, even when the needle would be placed into her wrist, hurting her, would just touch my heartstrings completely. When we would leave her chemo treatments and go to her home I would stay with her the first week. This was probably the most painful time for me and for Kehlie, her youngest daughter, because we saw how quickly she began to lose her hair. We would whisper and point to her head from behind her and then walk away feeling such sadness. The one thing Kehlie and I found out after the fact was that Pami heard our whispers and never said a word.

Some wonderful things I experienced as a caregiver was encouraging Pami, making her laugh, giving her food and drink to strengthen her, making sure she was kept warm and comfortable, and walking beside her on the sidewalk to give her some exercise. I would fluff the pillows for her to lay her cute little bald head on when she would go to sleep. I also wanted to make sure she had good hygiene.

I considered it such an honor to be with my daughter in the roughest times of her entire life. A mother's love runs so deep for her child, regardless of how old her child might be. Mom is there for her, no matter what.

*****

Written by: Dave Wyatt, father

Well, let's see if I can explain or express what I felt when I was told my daughter had cancer. I was surprised and disappointed. I had already been praying to God, therefore I felt anger. I felt I should pray more, but maybe I was just a bit short of faith at that time. However, Jesus does understand feelings and emotions. Seeing our daughter going through the many tests, the many doctor visits, surgeries and chemo treatments, as well as the long time it took to restructure what was lost, is both a lesson in trust and faith that she will be fine.

I will say, I had many talks with God. Hebrews 4:14-16 was brought up many times. I can now say God is working His plan and is using Pami for His glory. When anyone is really put to a test, a real test, you realize your many weaknesses and your strengths. Pami came out strong in her faith in God. I love her deeply.

*****

Written by: Dana Cevallos, sister

When my sister asked me to share my thoughts on caregiving, I considered it an honor. No one wants to get that dreadful call with, "You have cancer." Although I have never received a call like that, I did receive the call from my sister saying, "I have cancer." Fear is the best word I can use to describe how I felt because immediately your mind goes to losing that person. I guess I forgot what a mighty God I serve. I knew in that moment I was going to be there for her in any way possible. It would be a blessing for me, for sure. Caring for my sister was easy. I would sit in a chair and Pami would lie on the couch and try to watch a movie, but the minute it started she would be asleep – precious!

Walking past her from behind and seeing a good amount of hair on the back of her shirt that she didn't know was there – that was hard. And I didn't have the heart to tell her. Seeing her wiped of all of her energy, and she has a lot, was hard. Caring for her, easy.

I cared for my paternal grandparents up until their death, and I enjoyed every moment of it. Seeing someone suffer is never easy, but knowing that just being there might help a little bit is a wonderful feeling. Sometimes it's just sitting there in silence, sometimes it is laughing so hard you pee your pants, and sometimes it is crying together. Sometimes it is driving down the street and barking like dogs and having people look at you like you are crazy (we are used to that, though).

Slipping into bed with my sister after her husband goes to work so I can be close enough to hear her if she needed anything were moments to remember. Caregiving is a selfless, rewarding act. It reminds you that this life isn't just about you but about others as well.

The Bible says in 1 Thessalonians 5:11: *"Therefore encourage one another and build one another up, just as you are doing."* Philippians 2:4 says: *"Let each of you look not only to his own interests, but also to the interests of others."* Sometimes, caregiving takes you out of your comfort zone because it is never easy to watch others go through such difficult times, but that is what we are called to do. Life is short and we should count our blessings and remember that there is always someone out there who needs help. They need our care. They need you to give of your time.

Laughing is a great medicine. God gave us the gift of laughter, and let me just say, my sister and I put it to great use. I love you, Sister.

*****

Written by: Danny Wyatt, brother

All I can say is I have never witnessed a person going through cancer who had such a great attitude as you have.

*****

Written by: David Lee Wyatt, brother

Pami and I have always had a close bond, a bond that time, distance, nor could prison walls ever break. Since I was a little boy, separation was something that Pami and I would have to face against our will. However, when weekends came our parents, my brother, and Pami would come to pick me up and we would spend time together. I can still remember my sweet little angel Pami embracing me so tightly and being so excited to see me. I can remember to this day being behind the bushes and Pami making me mud pies. I probably thought she was the devil rather than my angel at that point!

Then our teen years came along, and I am sorry to tell you that I was still in and out of the beautiful home that I lived in with my parents, my brother, and three sisters. I had been making bad choices that led me to live on the streets and my stealing often times landed me in juvenile hall. When I was on the run I faced scary situations and it was my angel, Pami, who I would run to for comfort, love, and prayer. There were times when a police helicopter would be flying over her school trying to locate me and I would go to her class and tell her to come outside and she would. She would put her loving arms around me, pray for me, and plead with me to turn myself in to the authorities and

139

to allow Jesus to lead my life. Well, here we are many years later and once again I am ashamed to share with you that I am in prison for life.

I can remember the day I called my parents and my mom told me that Pami, my sister, had breast cancer. My heart dropped and suddenly I felt fear overtake me like I never felt before. *I can't lose my angel!* And when I say she's my angel, it is so true. I know that my Father Jehovah has appointed her to look over me for reasons I don't yet understand. Pami has been awakened in the middle of the night by a sharp pain in her belly and God let her know that I needed her. So, she began praying and the attack from the devil stopped and I was able to speak clearly. I prayed and rededicated my life to Christ in the middle of that night, the very same hour Pami prayed for me.

As you can see, I am very close to Pami. I was devastated the day I was notified of her cancer. I prayed and cried. I asked God to spare Pami's life and take mine instead. Every time I called Pami, my angel, she would sound so strong, joyful, and at peace as though nothing was wrong. She was facing death and was not even shaken because of her faith in Jesus Christ. Pami told me that death is only a shadow and it is not to be feared because once you pass through, you will be in heaven. At least this is how I interpreted what she said. However, my point here is that Pami is such a beautiful and rare woman of faith. She is courageous, humble, patient, kind, loving, thoughtful, wise, funny, and so much more even when facing death.

I wanted to share with you because I want everyone to know that my angel is a strong solider for Jesus Christ and she is cancer free, healed completely, and uses her life now to reach out to others going though cancer.

I have a tattoo that is a beautiful pink ribbon and underneath the ribbon it says, "My Angel." This is for Pami, who tears up every time she sees it.

Thank you for allowing me to share my heart from the cells of prison. However, I am free in Christ as I write this letter and will spend eternity with my sister, Pami, and many of you reading this.

*****

Written by: Lisa "Tiny" Duke, sister-in-law

I can recall the day that Doug, my husband, and I had been told that Pami had to get a biopsy. I didn't think that God would allow Pami to have cancer. On the day we were told she did in fact have breast cancer my first thought was *why?* Why would God do this to such a faithful, loving woman? Immediately, I felt fear set in and felt sick to my stomach. I was worried about how we would do life without Pami. I didn't have much faith. Then God spoke to me and reminded me of 2 Timothy 1:7: *"For God hath not given us the spirit of fear, but of power, and of love, and a sound mind."*

It was very hard to see this happen in my family, but what was so amazing was to see Pami with her faith in God and His Word. I would go over and sit while Pami would be resting; I think she felt good knowing someone was there. I would always bring her favorite tea or a burrito for her to enjoy.

One day, while I was watching Pami sleep, I remember

what God told me when we had a group prayer at their house. God told me that He did not give this to Pami, but He chose her because He had big plans for her. He chose her because of her love and faith in Him and I see her now, five years later and say to myself, "Wow, look at how she is doing now!" Michael, Pami, their children, and grandchildren have all given the glory to God, as do all of us! John 14:27: *"My peace I leave with you, not as the world gives, give I unto you. Let not your heart be troubled, neither let it be afraid."* This is exactly what the family did. I love you, Pami.

✱✱✱✱✱

Written by: Doug Duke, brother-in-law

The moment my wife, Lisa, and I got the news of Pam's diagnosis faith rose up inside me and I said, "No!" Pam has the victory in Jesus! Pam and I were both raised in churches that sang old hymns. The old songs still ring forth God's truth today just as the day they were written; they are full of God's promises.

So I made it my mission to call Pam when the Holy Spirit prompted me and I would sing to her. If she didn't answer then I would sing the song on her voicemail. *"Standing on the promises of Christ my King, through eternal ages let His praises ring! Glory in the highest I will shout and sing, standing on the promises of God!"* Amen! This was the way God showed me how to minister to her.

The best part for me was when I would get a response by her finishing the song. It made my heart happy because I knew it encouraged her and made her remember God's

Word through song (not that she was not already praising Him). Plus, I knew that it made her giggle because I can't sing!

There were so many wonderful friends and family members that stepped up to help. Scripture reminds us that the joy of the Lord is our strength and that a merry heart does good like medicine. When you are going through the battles of life remember: *"turn your eyes upon Jesus, look full in His wonderful face and the things of earth will grow strangely dim in the light of His glory and grace."* I haven't stopped making a joyful noise to the Lord for Pam. I love you, Pam.

*****

Written by: Josie Monica Guerrero, sister-in-law

The funny thing is I don't feel like I helped *you*. I feel like you helped *me* by watching you fight cancer with such strength and courage! You never turned against your God, or anyone else for that matter, and your testimony blew me away when I listened to you share. I left that place feeling so proud and honored to have you in my life. Because of how you fought this battle, I know I can fight any battle that may come up in my life. Thank you for showing me what strength, courage, and love can do. I love you my sister and my friend.

Chapter 23

HEAR ME ROAR

"Give thanks to the Lord,
for he is good;
his love endures forever."
1 Chronicles 16:34

There are times and seasons in our life that we must not wait for someone else to encourage us and we need to take time to encourage ourselves. As I mentioned earlier, I am reminded of the woman in the Bible with the issue of blood. She told herself if she could only touch the hem of His garment she would be healed. She dragged her tired and hurting body out into the crowds to touch Jesus. She didn't wait for someone to come get her and "drive her there" or wait until she felt strong enough to do something, she herself went out to into the crowds, the mass of people, and touched the hem of His garment. We must take time to encourage ourselves, as well. We can't be moved by our situation, by what our eyes see, or how our body feels. That doesn't mean we don't use wisdom. I am simply saying if we were moved by how we feel all the time we would just stay in bed and never get out. We need to stir ourselves up. We need to push through. We need to speak life over ourselves, as well as our situations.

I had to speak to myself. I told myself to get up and take a bath. I told myself to get my scripture cards out and read what I had written down. I told myself to get out of bed and go to the couch. On better days I told myself to get in the car and go to the grocery store. I told myself it was okay to go out to lunch and laugh with a friend. Often times, when we are surrounded by our family and friends, it is easy to be encouraged by them, but when we are alone and the enemy comes roaring in our ears and trying to defeat us, we must take a stand.

We must roar back. We must learn who we are in Christ. Who we are in Christ is not based on how we feel; it is based on who He is and what He has already done for us. He paid the price. We can walk in that freedom, in that liberty, that He so freely gave to us. Is it hard to do sometimes? Yes, very hard. I am not saying this because it was easy for me, it was just necessary for me.

As I read these scriptures over myself throughout this journey I realized that my fear was replaced with His supernatural peace. I knew with a complete, unshakeable belief and assurance that my God had rescued me. I didn't know how He would do it, only that He did. Whether that meant healing me physically or taking me home to be with Him, I was no longer afraid. I am His and nothing can change that. Not cancer, not chemo, and not death. Yes, death could claim me and my cancer riddled body, but it could never touch my cancer free soul or my cancer free spirit.

The Lord promised He would never leave me nor forsake me and He never has, and I know He never will. I am forever grateful for all He has done and that He is always with me no matter how things may look physically. As Jeremiah 29:11 says, *"'For I know the plans I have for you,' declares the Lord, 'plans to prosper you and not to harm you, plans to give you hope and a future.'"*

These are a few of the scriptures I stood on during this challenging but growing season.

- Let us encourage ourselves!

    o 1 Samuel 30:6b: *"But David strengthened himself in the Lord his God."*

- When I began to waiver in my faith, I would go to this verse and encourage myself.

    o Romans 4:20: *"he did not waiver at the promise of God through unbelief, but was strengthened in faith, giving glory to God."*

- Whenever the devil throws something at us, we need not lose our hope. Always hold on to hope. Keep hope alive on the inside of you.

    o Romans 8:31: *"What then shall we say to these things? If God is for us, who can be against us?"*

- I had to replace my fear with faith almost daily. Refuse fear. FEAR = False Evidence Appearing Real. Fear says we are powerless; faith tells us we are victorious!

    o 2 Timothy 1:7: *"For God did not give us a spirit of fear but of power and love and a sound mind."*

- He *never* leaves us, ever!

  - Isaiah 41:10: *"Fear not for I am with you; be not dismayed for I am your God. I will strengthen you, yes, I will help you. I will uphold you with my righteous right hand."*
  - Isaiah 41:10 (MSG): *"Don't panic, I'm with you. There's no need to fear for I'm your God. I'll give you strength. I'll help you. I'll hold you steady, keep a firm grip on you."*

- He is *my* healer! He is *your* healer!

  - Psalm 41:3: *"The Lord will strengthen him on his bed of illness; you will sustain him on his sick bed."*

- He is our strength to get through our dark days.

  - Habakkuk 3:19: *"The Lord God is my strength; He will make my feet like deers feet and He will make me walk on my high hills."*

- It is a shadow and shadows don't live, they only exist. I must remember to not camp in this valley of the shadow of death or fear evil. He comforts me and protects me and leads me through this season.

  - Psalm 23:4: *"Yea, though I walk through the valley of the shadow of death, I will fear no evil; for you are with me; your rod and your staff, they comfort me."*

- I realized that I couldn't possibly understand what I was going through, but I will choose to trust in His ways always.

    o Proverbs 3:5-6: *"Trust in the Lord with all your heart and lean not on your own understanding. In all your ways acknowledge Him, and He shall direct your paths."*

- I love this – He turns my heartbreak valley into a gateway of hope! I feel so encouraged reading this!

    o Hosea 2:15: *"My valleys of troubles into a gate way of hope."*
    o Hosea 2:15 (MSG): *"I'll turn heartbreak valley into acres of hope."*

- I constantly would lose heart unless I made a conscious decision to believe and He encouraged my heart!

    o Psalm 27:13-14: *"I would have lost heart, unless I had believed that I would see the goodness of the Lord. Wait on the Lord; be of good courage, and He shall strengthen your heart. Wait, I say, on the Lord."*

- See, my expectation was not in anything other than God Himself. He is my healer and my constant companion through it all. When I would lose my way I would remind myself, *keep your eyes on God*!

- o Psalm 62:5: *"My soul, wait silently for God alone, my expectation is from Him."*

- Singing praises lifted my heart and my head. I love to sing His praises; it makes me feel lighthearted once again!

  - o Psalm 35:28: *"And my tongue shall speak of your righteousness and of your praise all the day long."*

- So many times my flesh would fail me and my body would feel weak. I would remind myself of His word and feel refreshed as He strengthened my heart. He is my portion forever!

  - o Psalm 73:25-26: *"Whom have I in heaven but you? And there is none upon earth that I desire but you. My flesh and my heart fail; but God is the strength of my heart and my portion forever."*

- I love this scripture. I sang thanks to God and reminded myself of His faithfulness. I would declare His word over my situation even when I didn't "feel" it and soon I would experience His peace so deep within me!

  - o Psalm 92:1-2: *"It is good to give thanks to the Lord, and to sing praises to your name, o most high, to declare your loving kindness in the morning and your faithfulness every night."*

- When I was feeling really low I had decided to stand on this scripture. It encouraged me. It made me realize that I wanted to have His character. I wanted to hold on to His hope knowing that hope never disappoints. I needed to hold on to that hope. I would not let go. I rejoiced knowing He had given me the Holy Spirit!

  o Romans 5:3-5: *"We glory in tribulations, knowing that tribulation produces perseverance and perseverance, character, and character, hope. Now hope does not disappoint, because the love of God has been poured out in our hearts by the Holy Spirit who was given to us."*

- I especially love the New Living Translation; it seems to speak my language. Because of His Word, I have come to know so personally and so intimately that my God will not ever leave me nor forsake me. I can't put into words how that encourages me. Keep your eyes on the prize. Look at the promise as you walk through your journey and remain passionate, persistent, and positive. It is not easy and you will have down days. However, through Christ you can walk out the journey that you are on. We can become very negative when we lose our perspective. You *are* an overcomer. You *are* victorious. You *are* beautiful. You are incredibly and deeply loved by a gentle and fierce God. He lavishes you with His love and His grace every day.

  o Deuteronomy 31:6: *"Be strong and courageous. Do not be afraid or terrified*

*because of them, for the LORD your God
goes with you; he will never leave you nor
forsake you."*

- ○ Deuteronomy 31:6 (NLT): *"So be strong and
courageous! Do not be afraid and do not
panic before them. For the LORD your God
will personally go ahead of you. He will
neither fail you nor abandon you."*
- ○ Isaiah 40:8: *"The grass withers and the
flowers fail, but the word of our God
endures forever."*
- ○ Philippians 1:6: *"Being confident of this, that
He who began a good work in you will carry
it on to completion until the day of Jesus
Christ."*

Chapter 24

MY CAREGIVERS SPEAK OUT

"And now these three remain;
faith, hope and love.
But the greatest of these is love."
1 Corinthians 13:13

Caring for a loved one who has cancer often results in an ongoing time crunch. Caregiving responsibilities compete for the time required for tasks such as home maintenance, work, paying the bills, and taking care of one's own health.

Caregivers can't ignore their own needs, although that is usually the first thing people forget about when they are caring for their loved one. Caregivers can succeed without becoming exhausted by asking others for help and using a variety of strategies to stay organized.

In this chapter you will find personal stories from some of my amazing caregivers. I asked my caregivers to share a word with you to let you know you are never alone. I have been blessed beyond words to have amazing caregivers, people who love me for me. People who gave of their time when time was so hard to find. People who brought my family and me dinner constantly, praying over the food as they were cooking it. People who brought me lunch just to be sure I would try to eat. People who just sat with me while I slept so I would not be alone. Each and every one of my caregivers made me see that I am loved and I am special. I am important to them, so much so, that they put things on hold to attend to my needs during the hardest season of my life.

*****

Written by: Linda Westrick

"Caregiver" should not be a label. It is not something you do; it is who you are! My pastor has said over and over again, "Love is personal self sacrifice; the giving of oneself for the betterment of someone else." We care for those we love.

There are many levels of caregiving, and many things that factor in how much you are willing to give of yourself. For example, there are neighbors who you may cook an occasional meal for or run an errand, and family members that, even though your relationship with them is not very close, you feel a familial obligation to care for. You love them, but you feel inconvenienced doing the task. And then, there are people for whom you would lay down your life for.

It may be hard to understand my commitment towards Pam without first a little history of our background. Pam was my answered prayer for a friend and I hers. We have been friends for over thirty years. For our relationship, I think the word "friend" somehow is not enough. So, when Pam called and told me she had breast cancer, there was no doubt I would do anything to be there for her and be the friend she needed me to be during that time. Let me share a few things I have learned while being a caregiver to two very important people in my life who battled cancer - Pam, and my mother.

Time is Invaluable

Over the thirty years of our friendship, Pam developed many relationships and had many people in her life to care for her while she was ill. Because of this, my caregiving role was fairly small, but I learned that giving any amount of time was invaluable. Giving your time for someone else is probably the hardest thing to do. In our culture we feel the expectation to fill up every minute of our day. I remember sitting with Pam one evening while her husband and family were away. She was exhausted and weak from treatment and fell asleep on the couch while we were watching a movie. I was content in knowing she felt comfortable and safe enough with me to sleep soundly while I was there. There were no expectations to my visit — just my time and presence.

I did not and could not understand everything Pam was going through. One afternoon, she was getting ready for me to take her shopping and her hair was falling out in clumps. With all good intentions I said to her, "Why don't you just shave your head? It's just hair; it will grow back." She started crying! How could I understand the struggle she faced? To me, losing your hair was a temporary situation; to her, it was. . . .even now I do not know. But you don't need to know or understand. Just be there. Your presence is enough; it is everything!

Prayer is Vital

A crucial piece of caregiving (and life!) is prayer. When Pam was battling breast cancer, many of us would gather together and pray for Pam and her family before any major appointment. Lifting her up in prayer was a vital component in helping Pam face her situation with courage. Prayer reassured Pam and her family that they were not alone.

My role during Pam's battle with cancer was a couple of years ago. Between then and now, my mother became very, very ill. The doctors had to remove a large cancerous tumor from her colon, and, due to previous health issues that compounded after surgery, she was unable to fully recover. She was in the hospital for 179 days facing life and death situations every day. Being a caregiver for my mom during this time was one of the most heart-wrenching things I have ever done.

Almost every day after work I went to the hospital to be with my mom and care for her any way I could. I ate my lunch in the car for six months and did not go home until after dark. I found that if I prayed in the car to and from the hospital, I had the strength I needed for that day, that moment. I know now that the *only* way I survived was because of my relationship with God and the supernatural strength that came from prayer. I would rehearse my favorite scripture, drawing strength and peace from its truth. Isaiah 41:13: *"For the Lord thy God will hold thy right hand, saying unto thee, Fear not; I will help thee."* Without God I could not have endured.

Your Presence and Support is Cherished

When my mom was in the hospital, her favorite thing was for me to crawl into her hospital bed with her and take a nap. She craved human touch and affection. How difficult it would be to lie in a bed alone for six months without the ability to hug someone or cuddle up next to them! Your presence and support as a caregiver, whether emotional or physical, brings a sense of healing and normalcy.

My family set up a rotation for hospital visits to give each of us time to care for my mom. Six months is a long time to be a caregiver. Even though I knew she was in good hands, I would still feel guilty for not being there. But, as a caregiver, you must remember to take some time away from the situation and keep in touch with the life going on around you. It's so very hard, but necessary.

Singing Praises Brings Strength

During my mother's illness, I could not think about my husband or my family. I couldn't dwell on the fact that I wasn't cooking dinner, I wasn't cleaning the house, and I was missing out on being a part of their everyday lives. I felt as if I lived in a cocoon, but for me personally, it was a necessary evil to separate those parts of my life. In order to stay strong enough to be there for my mom, I had to compartmentalize. The well-being of my mother was more important to me.

My husband and children supported me, but their support was one of silence. They did not voice their disapproval of me "not taking care of myself" but I felt it. For me, the situation I was going through with my mom was temporary – even if it was a long time!

My mom loved singing the old hymns! We kept a hymnal by her bed and sometimes we would flip through the pages and sing her favorites. It brought such peace to our souls.

Then the day came when the doctors said that there wasn't anything else they could do for my mom. When you have prayed all you can pray and still need more from God there is only one thing you can do, and that is sing. As she breathed her last breath my sister and I were holding her hands, singing, *"Holy Spirit you are Welcome in this Place."* I felt something brush past me from behind. It was so overwhelming. My sister said, "Do you feel that?" and I said, "Absolutely!" We had the privilege of helping usher my mom into Heaven with song. God's promise of peace is real; it filled the room that day.

Singing unto the Lord is sometimes all you can do. So sing!

Here are a few scriptures that brought me the peace and strength I needed.

- John 15:13: *"Greater love hath no man than this, that a man lay down his life for his friends."*

- Isaiah 41:13: *"For I the Lord thy God will hold thy right hand, saying onto thee, Fear not; I am with thee."*

- John 14: 27: *"Peace I leave with you, my peace I give unto you; not as the world giveth, give I unto you. Let not your heart be troubled, neither let it be afraid."*

*****

Written by: Vanessa Reynolds

When Pam first told me she'd been diagnosed with breast cancer I felt like I'd been stabbed in my heart. She and I had been friends for several years and I was immediately hit with fear. I've been a believer for many years, and I know how to do spiritual warfare, and yet my immediate emotion was fear. After fear came acceptance that this was an attack of the enemy and I'd need to prepare for a battle.

I believe the biggest area that a caregiver can help in is prayer. In Exodus chapter 17 we're told how the Amalekites were battling against Joshua and the children of Israel. As long as Moses had his arms raised with the staff of God in his hands, the Israelites were winning in this battle. However, as Moses's arms became tired, the Amalekites started winning the battle. It took two men, one on each side of Moses, Aaron and Hur, to help him. These men gave him a stone to sit on, and each one held up an arm all day long until sunset. These friends enabled

Moses to be victorious in holding the staff of God so Joshua and the Israelites could defeat the Amalekites. Many times, a caregiver is that unseen, background supporter that can help the sick win the battle. Without the caregivers in Pam's life, she would not have had the strength to defeat cancer and subsequently bless others through her ministry.

What does it take to hold up someone's arms and give them a rock to sit on as Aaron and Hur did for Moses? It takes faith, perseverance, humility, and love. The Bible tells us trials will come just as they came to Jesus. We're in a world where Satan is prince. He seeks to kill, steal, and destroy. We must realize and always remind our sick loved ones that the battle has already been won. The stripes that Jesus bore on Calvary's cross took care of all sickness and disease that this enemy may try to use against us.

We must edify our loved ones by speaking the truth when they're too weak to read the Word and their faith falters. We must persevere when our own physical bodies are tired and we simultaneously have trials of our own. We must humbly adopt a servant's heart, providing those necessities that our loved ones need, but are incapable of doing at this stage of their lives. Helping them continue to feed their bodies, take medication, bathe, clean their houses, and take care of their children. Love is the motivation and impetus for your acts at this time.

In order to give you must stay filled to the brim with His Word or you will quickly become depleted. Stay in the Word. Listen to praise music. Pray in the spirit. Remind yourself daily of the faithfulness of God. Come prepared to serve with joy in your heart and a smile on your face. Watch what you say, always speaking the truth of the

Word instead of the truth of what you see. Our tongues are powerful. God spoke creation into existence. Every act we do is initially preceded by a thought. We see in our minds and dwell on those cookies that we know we shouldn't eat long before we actually take the first bite. Therefore, see your loved ones healed, happy, and enjoying life in your mind and speak His Word regarding healing every day.

Mark 11:24 reminds us: *"Therefore I tell you, whatever you ask for in prayer, believe that you have received it, and it will be yours."* We must stay in faith always while caring for the sick. We must keep our faith strong to always be able to encourage the sick. Remember, God will show Himself strong because he is faithful. I praise God once again for His faithfulness in healing my friend, Pam. She is truly an example to the verse in Romans 8:28 that tells us that all things work together for good to those who love God.

This victorious battle against cancer took Pam to a new spiritual height in God. It gave her the confidence to write this book and share her testimony with women all over the world. I'm grateful that God allowed us to become friends, and that I would be used to play a part in her testimony.

Hebrews 11:1: *"Now faith is being site of what we hope for, and certain of what we do not see."*

*****

Written by: Diane Forfa

I remember vividly feeling like a deer in the headlights upon hearing the report that my dearest, forever friend Pam being diagnosed with breast cancer. It took time for God to get me through the mental and spiritual processing of this devastating news. Initially, I felt helpless and paralyzed with fear. I had anxiety over all the possible "what if's" that could lay ahead for Pam in her fight against cancer.

Simply put, I was faced with two options: do I continue in fear or do I choose to be in faith? If I remained in a state of fear and worry I knew in my heart I would be ineffective in helping support Pam the way I believed God called me to. Moving forward in faith would enable me to help Pam, whom I dearly love with all of my heart! God knows I desperately wanted to be able to help her in every way possible!

God is faithful! He helped me overcome the fear, anxiety, and worry I had been carrying regarding Pam's health. Early during Pam's battle I made a choice to continually stand firmly upon God's promises, no matter what and regardless of what things looked like in the natural. Making this conscious decision freed me from all the negative thoughts so I was able to move forward in faith and take action! Gathering for a time of dedicated prayer at the Espinosa home, I remember looking around the room where Pam and Michael's dearest friends had come together to support them. As I noticed what a diverse group we all were, God laid on my heart what I personally could do to assist Pam and her family. God creates all of us unique and equips each of us with individual gifts and strengths in different areas of service. There is not one gift that is superior to another. There was one thing we all had in common: we were all committed to love and support Pam and her family through their journey fighting cancer. Ask God how you can help your loved one best through the battle they are fighting.

At the close of the Espinosa's prayer meeting, I began recruiting a list of volunteers willing to help with preparing and delivering meals to Pam and her family. Being practical minded, I was able to assist in covering other needed tasks and details. Meal planning consisted of consideration of food preferences, number of family members to be fed, preferred drop-off times, a friend being present to answer the door while Pam was resting, containers being marked with names to be returned, etc. I kept an "old-school" paper calendar containing important details such as names and contact numbers of who was scheduled to bring which food on which days (so the Espinosa's didn't end up with pasta or chicken dishes three consecutive nights!). Keeping a calendar also aided me in making reminder calls to Pam's loved ones for the days they had signed up to make and bring meals. Here is a handy tool I wish I had back then: www.takethemeal.com is an online site where all the details can be orchestrated and it simplifies the entire meal planning process!

In addition to organizing meals, here are other practical ways to help your loved one in need: lining up volunteers to assist with driving to doctors' appointments, tests, chemo and radiation treatments; assisting with administering medications; housecleaning, errands, laundry, and grocery shopping. It helped to have a point-person in order to keep communication flowing. Also, a person designated to make telephone calls in order to keep loved ones updated with news from regular doctor visits, patient progress, and patient recovery. It was beneficial to set healthy boundaries with limited visiting times so Pam could rest when needed. Pam even had friends who were able to donate finances towards the rapidly growing medical expenses. Pam's friends all came together and helped in ways they were able to as needs arose.

When you are close to someone who is fighting for their life battling cancer you want nothing more than to be able to take away their pain and stop them from hurting. The best advice I can offer is to be present and available! Meaning, when you see a need do your best to fill that need! Try to avoid running away or keeping your distance because you don't know how to help. Just ask, reach out, and stay connected. Don't waste time feeling badly about things you can't do – just commit to do what you are able to do! Some people help through prayer, some through visits and gentle hugs, some through calls, some through cards, some with words of encouragement through email or texting, some by spending afternoons watching movies and keeping Pam company. Others would stop by with Pam's favorite iced tea or hot cocoa. Even though Pam, at times, would have little or no appetite, especially during chemotherapy treatments, the impact of having her loved ones present and loving her where she was at through in every stage made a world of difference in Pam's victorious recovery over cancer!

*****

Written by: Haydee Stoffel

I pray my words might be of service as testimony for anyone going through cancer or anyone who has a loved one suffering from any type of sickness. I pray that the Holy Spirit will guide my words as I remember this difficult time for my friend, and that I can put into words my experiences with my beloved friend, Pami.

As I look back, everything happened so fast. It seemed as if time had stopped; it was such a period of uncertainty for me. One day, I saw Pam at a church event and I noticed she had lost a significant amount of weight. I asked her how she was losing her weight, "Are you exercising?" With a big smile on her face, as always, she told me that she wishes that were true, but she had actually been sick and having stomach issues, and that's how she had lost weight. I didn't think anything of it because Pam always has a big smile on her face and always has a cheerful attitude, no matter what.

The next thing I knew, I found out that my friend has cancer. I never realized how much I loved my friend. I was hurting for her and I was scared. Who knew that I would learn so many lessons from her – lessons of strength, lessons of faith, and lessons of love? Pam always relied on the Word of God. She spoke the Word of God and taught me how to be a woman of God, even in the worst times a woman could go through. I remember thinking what a great example she was to me and so many others. I remember on her worst days God was right there with her, as well as her beloved husband, Michael. Pam and I would talk about her experiences in battling cancer and how God was her strength and her rock. Michael was also a source of strength for Pam. He was such an example of how a man should love his wife, just like Jesus loves the church; always protecting his Pam.

I was honored to be a part of their experience because I also felt loved by the trust they showed in me. Never underestimate what can happen when you love unconditionally. You might think you are helping someone but instead, God is helping you by teaching you to walk in this amazing feeling of love we all have inside of us. I wanted to shave my head with Pam. I wanted to wear a mask like she did when we went places. I wanted to be like the hero she was. But I couldn't because she was the one picking up her cross and walking like Jesus did on Calvary.

I remember leaving her house one day and coming home to my husband and screaming how much I hated cancer. I was so mad at cancer! It was as if cancer was the devil that was hurting my friend in the natural. How could she look so fragile and so weak, and yet be so strong? The Word of God is alive in my friend. Prayers work! She had so many people praying for her.

It's amazing what God did in her life! It has been a miraculous road and every step that she took I could see her holding on to her Jesus's hand.

******

Written by: Robin Durant

In July 2002 I received a call from my mom, which was not unusual as she called me daily. She called to tell me she discovered a lump in her breast. At that moment I felt a range of emotions – anxiety, fear of the unknown, and grief. I said to myself, "Robin, get a grip. You serve a big and mighty God." At that moment a peace flooded my spirit. Mom went to the doctor's and she was diagnosed with third stage breast cancer. She had a lump the size of a golf ball. This was the moment I realized I was going to be a caregiver and had no idea the journey I was about to embark on.

The Education

I had never been a caregiver or trained for the responsibilities I was about to face. I never anticipated I'd be in this situation. As a family caregiver for my mother, I faced a host of new responsibilities, many of which were unfamiliar and intimidating. I had to learn about breast cancer, how insurance works and does not work, handling medications, finances, home health aides, insurance forms, etc. At times, I was overwhelmed.

The Journey

My mom started out with many chemo treatments. As the chemo treatments went on, it began to take a toll on her physically. The hair loss and lack of energy was difficult to endure. Mom was such an independent and strong woman and chemo was stripping her of that. Then she started radiation, which put her in ICU. As a result, I found myself at a crossroad. I was working full-time and caring for Mom. Her care now required so much more being in ICU. I had to make the decision to take a leave of absence from work. I struggled with the guilt of caring for my mom and the responsibility of helping to provide for my four kids and husband. I thank God my husband and family was with me 100% and supported me though the tough decisions.

All through this journey I believed God for a miracle that he would heal my mom. I struggled when she would have setbacks. Mom had a brief window where she began to improve but the cancer just continued to spread and the doctors told me they had done all they could. They advised me to take her home. She had maybe six months to live. It was difficult ordering a hospital bed to be delivered to my home, setting up home care, once again struggling with insurance coverage. One of the most difficult things was to make funeral arrangements and pick out a casket for someone who was still alive. I took my mom home and just cherished the last days I had with her. We spent three weeks with her before she graduated to heaven. I always told my mom it was an honor to care for her.

Words of Encouragement

We serve an amazing and righteous God. Through this journey we had hoped for a miracle healing on this earth. God had other plans for my mom. The beautiful thing was that she received her healing when she passed from the earthly realm into the spiritual realm. You see, cancer had to bow before the King of Kings and Lord of Lords! Amen! Caregiving is a time-consuming, emotionally draining, and physically exhausting job. So, no matter what level of care you are going through, God will give you the strength and ability to endure. Just trust in Him. Build a strong support system behind you. Don't try to be a hero; rely on family and friends who are willing to step in and help.

When Pam told me she had breast cancer it was like pulling a scab off an old wound. It brought back all the feelings and emotions of caring for my mom. I knew I had to deal with that and be strong for Pam. Pam has an amazing family and network of friends supporting her. I knew my role would be limited, but a powerful one.

The Lord spoke to my heart and I immediately knew I was to be a listener, encourager, and prayer warrior, consistently standing in the gap on her behalf. I was also called to pray for her husband, Michael, for strength and endurance. There were days when it was really hard for her and I was able to go to her house and just listen and pray. As caregivers, never forget no role is too small. Every prayer, every meal, every word of encouragement is worth its weight in gold! It was and always will be an honor to be there for my friend, Pam.

Shirley Lorraine Romaine 1937-2003

Chapter 25

PRACTICAL TIPS AND RESOURCES

"How much better to get wisdom than gold,
to get insight rather than silver."
Proverbs 16:16

How to inform family and friends of your cancer diagnosis is tough and very heart-wrenching. I found this to be a huge struggle when I was first diagnosed. I tried to convey that I had cancer while offering hope that I would be okay. Everyone reacts differently, but I found that it was best for me to have as much information as possible when I addressed my loved ones. I have dedicated this chapter to help you with practical tips and good resources as you walk this journey out. I pray it helps you and encourages you to know you are not alone. There have been many amazing, strong, determined, and courageous women who have gone before me and you. You also are an amazing, strong, determined, and courageous woman, and I am honored to walk this journey out with you.

Try to have as much information as you can about the type of cancer you have and what type of treatments are available to you. It may be best to inform immediate family members and close friends in person, if possible. Your family and close friends love you and want to be there to assist in any and every way possible. Don't be afraid to show your fear of the unknown. Allow your family and close friends to embrace you. Don't be surprised if other friends disappear during your cancer experience; it may be too overwhelming and scary for them. Once your immediate family and close friends are notified then there are plenty of social media outlets that can assist in keeping others informed or private blog sites, such as LotsaHelpingHands.com and CaringBridge.org.

Many will ask what they can do to help you. If you are like me, that is very hard to answer. I did not know what to expect, and therefore I did not know how to answer. Now that I have walked this out I have some ideas that helped me, and some that didn't, but are all great ideas.

- Cleaning house
- Doing laundry
- Ironing
- Running the vacuum
- Doing dishes
- Assisting with bathing
- Doing yard work
- Preparing meals, such as lunches, snacks, etc.
- Straightening out the fridge
- Giving rides to appointments
- Separating junk mail from personal mail
- Taking children to school or activities
- Taking kids out for a treat
- Caring for the pets
- Helping write thank you cards

- Assisting with treatment related paper work
- Keeping others updated (e.g., sending emails to keep everyone informed, scheduling assistance)
- Simply relaxing with you

Things to remember when you are feeling down:

- This too shall pass.
- You are *not* a statistic.
- The day is coming when cancer will not dominate your thinking, time, energy, or your life.
- You're not in this alone. You are surrounded by people who love you.
- There are still things to be grateful for.
- A year from today, this will all be behind you.
- You are probably facing the hardest thing you will ever have to deal with. So, it can only get better from here.

Empower yourself:

- Try to eat small meals. I had to eat whatever I could when I had some kind of an appetite.
- Do not force yourself to eat when you are feeling nauseated.
- Consume foods and beverages that are considered easy on the stomach, such as ginger ale, dry crackers, or toast.
- Limit your fluid intake while eating.
- Do not lie flat after eating for at least two hours, if you can.

- Keep Ensure nutritional shakes on hand. I often times would drink them when I could not bring myself to eat.
- Avoid caffeine and alcohol, food with strong odors that may make you feel nauseated, and spicy or greasy foods.
- I found that white Tic-Tacs helped my nausea. Keep them in the bathroom, next to your bed, or by the couch.
- Engage in relaxation exercises or activities. It will relieve stress and can decrease nausea and vomiting.
- Put music on, it helps relax you. I would put on praise and worship music; it encouraged my soul and brought me joy.

Good things will happen as a result of chemotherapy:

- Thick, lush hair will replace your old hair (most likely)
- Lavish curls will replace your straight hair (most likely)
- You will never take the hair on your head, eyebrows, nose hair, eye lashes, or pubic hair for granted.
- When something goes wrong and you say, "It could be worse," you mean it!
- No more hair on your legs (in some cases)
- No more hair under your arms (in some cases)
- Your skin will look younger.
- You can say, "Sorry, I'm just not up to it," even if you are, for a least the next several months.

- You'll never wish you didn't have an appetite.
- You won't take everyday things for granted.

Useful Resources:

- American Cancer Society
  (800) 227-2345 / cancer.org
- Cancer and Careers
  Cancerandcareers.org
- CancerCare
  (800) 813-4673 / cancercare.org
- LIVESTRONG Foundation
  (855) 220-7777 / livestrong.org
- National Cancer Institute
  (800) 422-6237 / cancer.gov
- Family Caregiver Alliance
  (800) 445-8106 / caregiver.org
- National Alliance for Caregiving
  www.caregiver.org
- NeedyMeds
  needymeds.org
- Partnership for Prescription Assistance
  (888)477-2669 / pparx.org
- Susan G. Komen for the Cure
  (877) 465-6636 / komen.org
- Young Survival Coalition (Under 40 Years Old)
  (877) 972-1011 / youngsurvival.org

A Good Read:

Any Day with Hair Is a Good Hair Day: How to Get Through Cancer and Get On with Your Life (Trust Me, I've Been There)

By: Michelle Rapkin

What cancer *cannot* do!

Cancer is so limited...

It cannot cripple LOVE

It cannot shatter HOPE

It cannot corrode FAITH

It cannot destroy PEACE

It cannot kill FRIENDSHIP

It cannot suppress MEMORIES

It cannot silence COURAGE

It cannot invade the SOUL

It cannot steal eternal LIFE

It cannot conquer the SPIRIT

Cancer Awareness Colors:

All cancers – Lavender

Appendix – Amber

Bladder – Marigold/Blue/Purple

Brain – Grey

Breast – Pink

Carcinoid – Zebra Stripe

Cervical – White

Childhood – Gold

Colon – Dark Blue

Esophageal – Periwinkle

Gallbladder/Bile Duct – Kelly Green

Head and Neck – Burgundy

Hodgkin's Lymphoma – Violet

Kidney – Orange

Leiomyosarcoma – Purple

Liposarcoma – Purple

Leukemia – Orange

Liver – Emerald

Lung – Pearl

Lymphoma – Lime

Melanoma – Black

Multiple Myaloma – Burgundy

Ovarian – Teal

Pancreatic – Purple

Prostate – Light Blue

Sarcoma/Bone – Yellow

Stomach – Periwinkle

Testicular – Orchid

Thyroid – Teal/Pink/Blue

Uterine – Peach

Honors Caregivers – Plum

ABOUT THE AUTHOR

Pam has been married to her loving and supportive husband Michael, 34 years. She is the mother to three beautiful children and Grammy to four amazing little ones.

She is a full time minister for God; preaching in Women's Ministries and Marriage Conferences. She is a broadcaster for The Holy Spirit Broadcasting TV and Radio Network (HSBN), encouraging millions of others on her program entitled, **"Encouragement for Today."**

Pam was diagnosed with breast cancer in September 2009 and this journey has given her a renewed understanding of God's healing power, grace and love.

Pam shares the Word everywhere she goes and has traveled to the Philippines for missions, shares in other churches, conferences as well as women's retreats.

Pam has written a book titled *"Life Interrupted"*, it is a hard to put down book based on her challenges and victories with breast cancer.

Her bubbly personality, love for Christ, and knowledge of excellence is evident in her daily walk. Everyone should have the opportunity to have this seasoned woman of God share her trials, her victories and her Jesus.

Cancer isn't funny but humor is healing. Singing praises in your midnight hour causes you to realize that there may be sorrow in the night but joy comes in the morning. As someone who has gone through breast cancer (mastectomy, chemotherapy, and reconstruction) and gratefully came out the other side, I have learned firsthand that laughter and praise has its place and it sure helps.

From going bald to losing twenty-five pounds the chemo diet way, humor and praise has been an effective weapon in my fight against this disease that is no respecter of persons. This is not to say that I laughed throughout my whole cancer experience; I didn't. This isn't to say that I sang praises every day, because I didn't. However, I often times found myself encouraging those who came by to cheer me up. I would put them at ease by asking them if they wanted to see my boob-less chest or my baldhead. Laughter helps, and so does talking to someone who's "been there."

My prayer is that this book will help someone who is going through breast cancer, and also help those who love them. Faith, hope, praise, and a good dose of laughter can make a great difference in the journey you are now experiencing. Sharing with other women helps diffuse the fear of cancer. Cancer is not a life sentence – it is merely a word.

I also hope this book will encourage women everywhere to get a mammogram today!

CONTACT INFORMATION

Encouragement for Today Ministries
P.O. Box 1833
Yucaipa, CA
92399
(909)797-1540

Website:
Encouragementfortodayministries.com

Email address:
Pam@encouragement-for-today.com

You would be blessed to see Pam
on her program called:
"Encouragement for Today"

at WWW.HSBN.TV
and on ROKU TV on the HSBN Channel.